SON OF PERDITION

THE MAGIC AND HUBRIS OF SIMON MAGUS

M.R. Osborne, M.A.

Foreword by Tony Hutchins

Second Edition

A catalogue for this book is available from the British Library

Copyright © M. R. Osborne 2022, 2025

All rights reserved. No part of this book may be reproduced, distributed, stored in a retrieval system, or transmitted in any form or by any means, including photocopying, recording, or other electronic or mechanical methods, without the prior written permission of the publisher, except in the case of brief quotations embodied in critical reviews and certain other non-commercial uses permitted by copyright law.
For permission requests, write to the publisher at the address below:

ISBN 978-1-0684008-6-5

Published by
Rose Circle Publications
P.O. Box 854
Bayonne, NJ 07002, U.S.A.
www.rosecirclebooks.com

About The Author

M.R. Osborne writes on Christian mysticism and Western esotericism. He is immersed in the study and practice of philosophical alchemy and Christian theo-philosophy.

Osborne is the author of several works, including ***The Threefold Anglican Ministry in the Writings of Thomas Cranmer, Richard Hooker and Jeremy Taylor; Martinez de Pasqually and the Office of the Holy Spirit***, and ***Son of Perdition: The Magic and Hubris of Simon Magus***.

In collaboration with Rose Circle Publications, he produced the first fully restored and complete colour reproduction of ***The Most Holy Trinosophia: A Book of the Dead***, drawing comparisons in his research between the origins of this mysterious manuscript and the Egyptian books of the dead.

Other Books by the Author

The Lessons of Lyons (Rose Circle Publications, 2021, ISBN: 979-88889566252021)

The Brazen Serpent: Chaos and Order (Rose Circle Publications, 2022, ISBN: 979-19479071952022)

The Most Holy Trinosophia: A Book of the Dead (Rose Circle Publications, 2021, ISBN: 978-19479071642022)

Pierre Fournie: What We Have Been, What Are And What We Will Become (Rose Circle Publications, 2022, ISBN: 979-88889689252023)

Allegory in Stone: A Short Study of the Shakespeare Monument (Rose Circle Publications, 2022, ISBN: 979-88879695412023)

Time Slip Phenomena: The Ghost of the Trianon, The Legend of Lucy Lightfoot and the Haunting of William Hogarth (Rose Circle Publications, 2023, ISBN: B0CJVT2DV2)2023)

Martinez de Pasqually: Treatise on the Reintegration of Beings (Rose Circle Publications, 2023, ISBN: 979-8-89034-491-52024)

The de Grainville Manuscripts (Rose Circle Publications, 2024, ISBN: 979-88926988322024)

The Alchemy of William Blake: The Three Principles of the Divine Essence and 'An Allegory on the Spiritual Condition of Man' (Rose Circle Publications, 2024, ISBN: 978-1-0369118-2-9)

The Threefold Anglican Ministry in the Writings of Thomas Cranmer, Richard Hooker and Jeremy Taylor (Whitestone Esoteric, 2024, ISBN: 978-1-0684008-8-9)

William Laud (1573-1645) Writings on the Church, Ministry and Sacraments (Rose Circle Publications, 2024, ISBN: 978-1-0684008-7-2)

Martinez de Pasqually and the Office of the Holy Spirit (Rose Circle Publications, 2025, ISBN. 978-1 0684008-9-6)

www.mrosborne.co.uk

"'Stranger,' said he, 'you are a fool, or else you know nothing of this country. Talk to me, indeed, about fearing the gods or shunning their anger? We do not care about Zeus or any of your blessed gods, for we are ever so much stronger than they. I shall not spare either yourself or your companions out of any regard for Zeus unless I am in the humour for doing so.'"
Homer, *The Odyssey*, Book IX

Contents

Foreword……………………………..…..11

Introduction……………………...……..17

1. Shim'on of Gitta……………..…..37

2. Shim'on of Bethsaida…………….53

3. Charism………………...…..…..65

4. The Standing One………………...99

5. Magic………..............……....113

6. Necromancy………………...……163

7. Son of Perdition………………...181

Concluding Remarks........................... 197

Bibliography......................................205

Index...207

Foreword

I first became acquainted with the author at the end of 2021, when a website containing past Societas Rosicruciana in Anglia (SRIA) papers momentarily went down. He sent in his award-winning paper on the "Lessons of Lyons" for uploading, and we have engaged one another in a lively correspondence ever since. I had recently read the author's *Brazen Serpent: Chaos and Order*, a book about Moses' raised serpent, the Nehushtan. I felt that book could have been written just for me, as it touches upon so many of the experiences and questions I have of life and the Quest. Indeed, the *Brazen Serpent* breaks new ground and breathes life back into that ancient, almost forgotten symbol. I had always thought of the Nehushtan as a thing in itself, but the book vastly broadened my thinking, particularly about the power of numbers, and links to the Ark of the Covenant, amongst other ideas. Most interesting.

    I asked the author why he had attributed the Sepher Yetzirah to the Tree of life – as I had never seen that equation before – as the name is given to the Book of Formation. It is literally *Etz Chaim*, Hebrew for the tree of life. Michael's response demonstrated a depth of thought, and reminded me why it is so worthwhile engaging in esoteric conversations. By tradition, Abraham described the paths as the *Yah-Sefer* (literally *Sefer Yetzirah*, "God's Branches"). This concept also appears in the sacred tree and nine worlds of Yggdrasil, and elsewhere in ancient mythology. I realised the strangest thing - that the Book of Formation does indeed mention the ten Sephiroth - albeit in passing and without naming them. In my mind I had fixated on the twenty-two letters of the Hebrew alphabet only. I did study the Sefer Yetzirah years ago but had totally forgotten that the "Ten Sephiroth of nothingness" is mentioned many times in the first part. Such insights, and the ease of their explanation are a hall-mark of this author. I likewise struggled to make a connection between the Beast of Geborah and the Beast of Revelation. The answer came in the conjoining of the paths of judgment and limitation in the fifth sefira, and the confluence of fiery water and mind concealed in nature as the essence of the twenty-third path.

Personally, I found myself perfectly in-tune with the author's thesis on the Divine Code as elucidated in The Brazen Serpent, and recalled my first summing up of the twenty-three triangular numbers. It also brought back to mind why Stifel used a twenty-three letter alphabet in his numerology. I had also once thought Stifel redundant because of his ill-judged prediction of the end of the world on 19 October 1533, but after reading The Brazen Serpent, I came to see that date as a code for the number of chaos concealed in nature by reason, of the formula $1+9+1+0+1+5+3+3=23$. Fascinating. It is an amazing book, one of a kind. Walking the serpent path now in SRIA ritual has so many connotations for me, thanks to it. The author kindly also sent me a hard cover volume of his version of *The Lessons of Lyons*, a magnificent tome containing the first English translation of many of the surviving notes made by the Élus Coên adepts in the mid-1770s.

I have also read his *Most Holy Trinosophia – A Book of the Dead*. As a result of our exchanges about these books and other related matters (for instance, we share a common fascination and synchronicity with the number twenty-three), he asked me if I would write a foreword to this, his latest book on Simon Magus. I must confess that I was only vaguely familiar with the subject of Simon Magus. I thought this would disqualify me from writing on it, but I rose to the challenge because of my deep conviction that all spiritual truth lies barely beneath the surface. I remember at one point

Michael asking me if I knew of an expert on ancient magic, not realizing then that this is the book he was researching. At the outset I must say the author has a gift for gently simplifying the concepts underlying complex topics – in particular Martinism – and he is one of the few who can make sense of the texts for ordinary readers, in the sense of shining a light on the material and extracting the intellectual bases underpinning them. Colin Wilson would have enjoyed writing this foreword and would have credited Michael with using "Faculty X" to go back in time and re-live events at the time of Christ. The author's descriptions of the Holy Land recalled to mind the year 1973, when I was working on an archaeological dig at the Temple Mount in Jerusalem. We had unearthed the entrance to a tunnel (Hezekiah's tunnel) previously discovered circa 1867 by Charles Warren. I was about to crawl in when the Yom Kippur war broke out. That is nearly 50 years ago now.

This present book about the magic and hubris of Simon Magus, and whether he fits into the archetype of a false messiah or antichrist, is an adventure of ideas in the spirit of Alfred North Whitehead. It will take you back in time to "see" with your imagination what was happening, so that you can come to your own conclusions. The mechanism of literary time travel is, in truth, the quotation of sources that are as contemporary as possible, together with a most interesting commentary and speculation.

A rich series of concepts are outlined – the Gnostic view of creation is explained very clearly, and in fact that seems to be the cosmology influencing our Simon, which certainly put him at odds with the Apostles, especially when they were spreading the gospel and recruiting followers. For the most part, Simon is largely treated sympathetically by the author, although he draws back from maintaining Simon was a victim of Christian 'politics' at the time. It seems we have to accept that there were magicians back then, and who did actually perform magic. On the one hand, we have Christ and his disciples performing miracles, and it seems Simon was perceived as a competitor. Peter and Simon may have held a magical battle in Rome. I did not know any of this until I read the book. Their antics in the Roman Forum feel like a circus to me – those with the best "tricks" gained more followers. I personally enjoy all the quotations in the book, as I am guilty of not being thorough in my own reading of the Bible – I have several versions but seem to use them for reference rather than reading. I have been missing out. The author mentions this aspect in his book too – how today we have lost touch with the stories in the Bible.

This book will be of great interest to all with inquiring minds, including Christian Freemasons and Martinists in particular. There is a Martinist theme running through this book too – very valuable in my view, because it is so clearly elucidated, unlike what we find in many Martinist texts themselves. There is a section on sex magic, as Simon and his followers were accused of orgies, and his consort Helena (or Helen) was the subject of what I would call vitriolic verbal abuse by Church writers. One can never be quite sure though. The discussion about the religious groups of the day is fascinating. Apart from Christ there were disciples of John the Baptist and, of course, Simon Magus and his followers in Samaria.

The author brings in some concepts that are probably of a later date – for example the Qliphoth, however I have to accept that parallel beliefs were possibly held much earlier and transmitted orally. That was how the ancient world worked. We do not really know when the Rabbis started conceiving the Kabbalah, and it may have been embedded in the very fabric of time and space and therefore known since man started walking on two legs. At least the author does not mention the modern idea of Qliphothic tunnels, which sound even less inviting than the paths.

Tony Hutchins
Wellington, February 2022

Introduction

At all times and places there is usually tension between the institutional, intellectual and mystical camps of organised religions.[1] The Anglo-Austrian theologian Friedrich von Hügel (1852–1925) highlighted this inherent conflict between the practical and mystical dimensions of religious practice, and which is no better illustrated than in the legendary encounter between Simon Magus and the fledgling Church of the first century.

The established religious order in the western world is giving way to a resurgence in mysticism, magic and the revival of neo-pagan systems. The rapid decline of organised Christianity has seen the advent of less dogmatic and restrictive social and spiritual conventions, permitting greater exploration and inquiry. However, the problem with the collapse of traditional religion is the vacuum this social phenomenon leaves in the spiritual lives of many – if not most - and which will be even more keenly felt as the twenty-first century progresses. Thus it seems Cardinal Newman's "second spring" of Catholic revival turned out to be eternal winter after all.

There are attendant risks in the mass abandonment of Christianity, and there is much to mourn about the loss of the common knowledge of the vitality and wisdom to be found in its mythology. Where once there was a flourishing shared knowledge of biblical lore, today there is precious little. For those who show an interest in specifically Christianised mysticism the need to revisit the fascinating cosmogony of the early Church is required almost from scratch, as it were,

---

[1] See von Hügel's *The Mystical Element of Religion as Studied in St. Catherine of Genoa and Her Friends* (1908)

if only because commonplace knowledge of its story is no longer part of our culture. In short, many readers will encounter the events and characters recounted in this book for the first time.

There is also the obvious question whether spirit and the spiritual realm exists, and if the material and ethereal worlds continue to exert their influence upon one another. For many, the corresponding collapse of Christianity in the west has left civilisation in danger of moral collapse, and they perceive therein a very real danger of something taking its place that is ultimately quite dangerous – by which I mean materialist atheism in its worst form. So we live in a state of imbalance at present, which in many ways is not dissimilar to the world the nascent Church found itself in two thousand years ago.

This is something of personal meaning to me, because as a young man I took up theology with a view to entering the ministry. An impression of this youthful period lingers - as if a footprint from over thirty years ago - in an attachment to Christianity, albeit in an obscure way that is now difficult for me to articulate. Perhaps it is best summed up by Gandhi's famous quip: "I like your Christ, but not your Christianity."

While I became less religious as the years passed, so I became more spiritual, and perennially curious as to the nature of God and the purpose of humanity. My own view, for what it is worth, is that society reflects upon itself a great loss in the decline of Christianity, yet there does remain a dwindling collective memory, sustained perhaps by an undefined yet perceptible sense of *zeitgheist*, nameless and misunderstood at best. Such memory will inevitably slip into history and cease to be, sooner or later.

Evolution is the process by which physical things change over time. It therefore necessarily fails to recognise the existence of spiritual evolution, because it cannot perceive or prove spirit exists through empirical processes. Yet alternative dimensions or planes - and the intelligent beings inhabiting them - almost certainly do exist. If so, then they might be able to influence physical nature in places where they are able to concentrate their powers. Such is the phenomena of the paranormal in summary, and which science cannot yet explain. There is no reason to suppose that human beings cannot also operate on a psychic level given the means to do so, and the question of magic therefore raises the question as to what, exactly, constitutes spirit.

Writing in 1930, the physical medium and novelist Dion Fortune attempted to explain this by reference to spirit as an "etheric force":

> "Occultists maintain that mind affects body by means of the etheric double ... The etheric double is primarily a body of magnetic stresses in the framework of whose meshes every cell and fibre of the physical body is held as in a rack. Intermediate between this and the dense physical body as we know it, there is what may be called the raw material out of which dense matter is condensed. This was called by the ancients, Hyle,[2] or First Matter, and by the moderns, Ectoplasm. It is this projected ectoplasm which produces the phenomena whenever physical manifestations are in question."[3]

Any reference to "ectoplasm" elicits ridicule and misunderstanding today, not least because of the well-publicised and incredulous fraud perpetrated by fake

---

[2] Matter, essence or substance, from the Greek noun οὐσία, *ousia*.

[3] Dion Fortune, *Psychic Self Defence*, 1930, p.22

mediums during the golden age of psychical research. Yet might this supposed cloud of viscous material - or something like it - be the vehicle through which supernatural entities exhibit perceptible form and interact with us?

For instance, the Greek noun οὐσία (*ousia* meaning substance) is formed from the feminine participle of the verb εἰμί (*eimí* meaning "I am"). We need hardly be reminded of the words of God in Exodus 3:14 from within the burning bush: "I AM who I AM, and thus you shall say to the children of Israel, 'I AM has sent me.'"). The occultist S. L. MacGregor Mathers once wrote that all of the transpositions for the sacred name of God convey an identical meaning, which is "to be."[4]

There is no reason why this *materia* should not exist as a product of energy like any other, and someday might be proved by science. For the present day sceptic, it will be noted that the natural transmutation of matter occurs in nature all the time. The most obvious example is the process of radioactive decay, when atomic nuclei emit high-energy particles and transform themselves into an entirely *different* element. This is not magic, it is nature, albeit nature being manipulated by the scientist as an outside power concentrating his will upon it. If we exchange the scientist for the mage, we are perhaps simply describing different sides of the same coin. Perhaps manipulation of nature is the sum explanation for all supernatural phenomena, at least of the variety that is able to influence the physical world.[5] One aspect

---

[4] Sl. L. MacGregor Mathers, *The Kabballah Unveiled*, New York, 1912, p.p.30-31

[5] "We have very little exact knowledge concerning these subtle forces which are the basis of both occult attack and spiritual healing, but we have good reason to believe that in their nature they are closely analogous to

to consider is whether the difference between magic and miracle resides in the arena of legitimacy, i.e. of what is deemed right or wrong, true or false, depending on our point of view. That in essence is the subject matter of this book, and summarises the core dispute between the Primitive Church and ancient magic.

A great deal has been written over the centuries about Simon Magus and his confrontation with the early Church, and it is now well over 130 years since G.R.S. Meade's seminal theosophic work on the subject.[6] A fresh look needs to be taken. The purpose of this book is to consider anew the character of Simon Magus as a potential candidate for a false messiah or antichrist within the context of his deeds and likely beliefs. We need to reflect upon the difference between miracles and magic in the Apostolic Age, and draw comparisons with the present-day sacralised worship of the Catholic Church.

The story of St. Peter's encounter with Simon the Sorcerer is suggestive of an historicity which is tantalising enough to cause one to dig deeper to seek its meaning, and what might have happened. The fascinating battle between Apostolic power and pagan magic is an incredible area for reflection and study. Thus, we shall look at the character and legend of Simon Magus afresh and rediscover the interaction of this fascinating man with the founding fathers of the Church.

This book is structured carefully to look at the historical evidence and the characteristics of the main protagonists. We will consider the doctrine of charism and the role of the Holy Spirit in the early Church, and

---

electricity. They are not inanimate forces, however, but have in their nature something that is akin to life, though of a low type." Op.cit. Fortune p.22

[6] G.R.S. Meade, *Simon Magus*, London, 1892

how this influenced the views of Simon and St. Peter, before turning to an exposition of the likely beliefs of the Simonian sect in the chapter on gnosis. Having built a suitable picture, we shall turn our attention to the magic of Simon Magus, and dedicate an entire chapter to the art of necromancy as practised in his time. Finally, we will consider Simon as a likely contender for the role of a false messiah or antichrist.

Magic

Magic is a difficult area for research because it takes so many forms and its workings can be complex. We are also at a particular disadvantage when considering ancient magic because most of the written books of spells were destroyed in antiquity, and what we are left with are glimpses of traditions preserved in the much later grimoires of the late Middle Ages. The reader is therefore asked to make use of their, his or her imagination so as to suspend incredulity, and to take the magic of Simon Magus seriously. Regardless of how fantastical or superstitious many of the apocryphal texts may appear to the twenty-first century mind, there will always be fragments of truth contained in them.

We must, to be fair, consider the possibility that Simon Magus was a fraudulent mentalist. We should also acknowledge that there is no proof connecting the Simon who appears in the New Testament Book of Acts with the man of that name described by Josephus, or the mage who contrived trouble for the Apostles in Rome. Yet, if we accept all of the various testimonies of his magic and likely identity at face value, then we encounter an adept magician able to use powerful polymorphic spells.

For example, when we consider the use of evocation magic by Simon to create objects out of nothing more than air, then we are witnessing the manipulation of nature from unseen sources that are consistent throughout the varied testimonies concerning him. Indeed, in the operative systems known to us as "black magic", there are offensive spells used to harm or even kill, connecting the sorcerer with quite specific groupings of disembodied entities exhibiting their own particular types of power.[7] One such example given in this book is that of the demon Lucifuge Rofocale, the chief emissary of the demonic gatekeepers. We will see just how dark the magic of Simon Magus may at times have been.

Yet there do remain many unanswered questions. For instance, what type of magic did Simon practise? Was it sympathetic or force magic? Was he reliant on devices and talismans, and were his practises goetic evocations of disembodied spirits, ghosts, angels, and demons? How might Simon have become an adept, and to what extent does his character reflect that desire?

It is, alas, impossible to answer these questions definitively, because the historical sources are scant and unreliable. It helps, however, to have a rough idea of the range of magical practise, and for this I am indebted to A. E. Waite's early twentieth century classic *The Book of Ceremonial Magic or The Book of Black Magic and of Pacts*. Notwithstanding its age, Waite's book has continued to influence many researchers for its breadth and sheer scope of information, indeed the late psychedelic researcher Terence McKenna cited Waite's *The Book of Ceremonial Magic* stating that:

---

[7] Said to be conducted through the "rays of the Dark Star", a form of magic using astrological workings aiding astral travel, evocation and divination. As such it was regarded as an unclean and illegitimate form of magic in Judaism.

"The syntactical nature of reality, the real secret of magic, is that the world is made of words. And if you know the words that the world is made of, you can make of it whatever you wish."

Waite himself recited a useful letter in *The Book of Ceremonial Magic* from one of his correspondents to provide an example of the generally accepted division between natural and occult magic (a description he was not personally in favour of). Notwithstanding Waite's reservations, the reader is urged to keep in mind this summary:

"Practical Magic is the science of the economy of spiritual dynamics and is concerned with those theurgic processes whereby he who has trained himself for the purpose can, by virtue of powers inherent in man's spiritual constitution (but undeveloped in the majority of mankind), enter into relations with the unseen intelligences to whom are assigned, in due order, the control of what are called natural forces. 'Ceremonial Magic' (*presumably not that of the Ceremonial Literature*) is Official Magic, in which the Magician, in connection with one or more assistants, acts as the delegate of an occult Fraternity, who, for some very important end, wish to communicate with beings of a higher order than usual. For this purpose, there is a recognised ceremonial, or rather there are two- the 'ceremonial of approach' and the 'ceremonial of the presence.' It is chiefly in the former that lights, fumigations, symbolic figures and numbers, and incantations occur, all of which have their use, either as credentials of authority or as weapons of attack and defence in the intermediate hostile region between the material and spiritual universe." (Waite, The Book of Ceremonial Magic , p. 32)

There is of course an opposite and well-established modern tradition of debunking all forms of magic (and spiritualism). Indeed, even in the time of Simon Magus, allegations of trickery, deceit and fraud were being made against him. For example, the notable English magician John Nevil Maskelyne (1839-1917) was keen on replicating magical demonstrations and exposing them as optical illusions without any supernatural merit whatsoever. One of his best-known performances was that of levitation, a form of magic which Simon Magus was said to have practised (and indeed which by legend led directly to his death). Maskelyne's trick used a contraption hidden from the audience. Nevertheless, even at the time there were critical challenges to Maskelyne's attempts to explain all magic as trickery or mentalism. One notable critic of Maskelyne was Thomas Colley, Archdeacon of Stockton in Warwickshire,[8] who successfully sued him for failing to replicate the visual manifestations of the well-known medium (and Anglican clergyman) Francis Ward Monck. So, we must suspend our judgment and enter into the mindset of the ancients, because this is the only way we can appreciate the remarkable but flawed man known to history as Simon Magus.

---

[8] "Archdeacon Colley had a glass topped coffin made; at one Sunday evening service, he started his congregation by climbing into his coffin in all his robes and was carried around the church. The reason for this was to demonstrate that he was not afraid of dying. The coffin was kept in his study and those who attended confirmation classes had to sit on it."
See www.ourwarwickshire.org.uk

The Bones of St. Peter

At university I stumbled across John E. Walsh's *The Bones of St Peter* (Walsh, 1982),[9] recounting the excavations conducted beneath the Vatican in the 1940s. I found his book riveting. The possibility that a team of excavators delving below St. Peter's Basilica had located the saint's relics fired up my imagination. The dig purportedly uncovered the original, first century ground level and the remains of an ancient cemetery situated near the Gardens of Nero. Since the location of St. Peter's burial was firmly fixed in local lore, ancient Christian graffiti led the team directly to the site. It was close to where the Apostle was understood to have been martyred during the Neronian Persecutions of AD 64.

The original fourth century basilica erected by the emperor Constantine was apparently built to accommodate this cemetery, and though only circumstantial evidence supports the claim that the relics found there are St. Peter's, it is tradition that he died near there. In the pseudepigraphal Acts of Peter it is said that Marcellus, "an illustrious man of Rome", abandoned Simon Magus to follow Peter "and took up his body secretly, and put it under the terebinth near the place for the exhibition of sea-fights in the place called the Vatican." (Acts of Peter ch.31). The Acts of Peter provide a potential source of information for the historical Simon Magus, with some scholars contending that material may date from as early as AD 200-210 (Schmidt, 1903, p. 1003).[10] Indeed, the Acts of Peter might incorporate fragments of earlier manuscripts. The main example of this is the crucifixion account for St. Peter. In any event, legend has it that Peter's skull was

---

[9] John E. Walsh, The Bones of St Peter, London, 1982
[10] According to Schmidt the Acts of Peter were composed between AD 200–210 at Jerusalem and Rome.

removed in the ninth century and later interred at the Archbasilica of St. John Lateran in Rome, together with the skull of St. Paul who died during the same persecution. The relevance for our purposes is the link between the historical Peter, Simon Magus and Rome.

The problem of course is that historical research simply yields further layers of circumstance and conjecture, albeit not unexpected for a period where the lowest born individuals left few if any records of their existence.[11] Like many seeking certainty in history, it is rarely found.

All Roads Lead to Rome

By happenchance a few years ago my wife and I stumbled upon the **church of** San Sebastiano Fuori le Mura along the Appian Way. Tired almost beyond endurance by the relentless walking caused by our inability to figure out the Roman bus service, we circumnavigated a group of youths kicking a football in the church courtyard. We were far from being in a spiritual frame of mind, and collapsed into the cool interior, close to the place where Peter is said to have rested on his flight from Rome.[12] The early twentieth-century biblical historian George Edmundson summarized the legend as follows (Edmundson, 1913):[13]

---

[11] While there is no evidence that Peter was in Rome in the New Testament, the first epistle of Peter mentions that "The church that is at Babylon, elected together with you, saluteth you; and so doth Marcus my son." 1 Peter 5:13

[12] Also in the Acts of Peter

[13] George Edmundson, *The Church in Rome in the First Century*, London, 1913

"His friends, so runs the story, had entreated the Apostle to save his life by leaving the city. Peter at last consented, but on condition that he should go away alone. But when he wished to pass the gate of the city, he saw Christ meeting him. Falling down in adoration he says to Him 'Lord, whither goest Thou?' And Christ replied to him 'I am coming to Rome to be again crucified.' And Peter says to Him 'Lord, wilt Thou again be crucified?' And the Lord said to him 'Even so, I will again be crucified.' Peter said to Him 'Lord, I will return and will follow Thee.' And with these words the Lord ascended into Heaven ... and Peter, afterwards coming to himself, understood that it was of his own passion that it had been spoken, because that in it the Lord would suffer. The Apostle then returned with joy to meet the death which the Lord had signified that he should die."

The beauty of an experience of this nature is that it is unexpected. Inside the church, we came across the marble slab of a pair of feet (not at all life-like) which are said to be casts of Christ's footprints. The significance of the encounter was not lost on me, and my thoughts immediately turned to the legend of St. Peter's showdown with Simon Magus in the Roman Forum. It is unknown if the legend encapsulates fragments of truth, but it probably does. If so, we can take a view as to whether Marcellus ever existed, or if Simon Magus travelled from Samaria to Rome via Cyprus.

Scholarship has become increasingly interested in the influence and role of magic in the New Testament period, not least because of the false assumption that it was forbidden by the *Halakhah* (the Jewish Law). By way of example, in the biblical books of Deuteronomy and Exodus we read:

> "There shall not be found among you anyone that maketh his son or his daughter to pass through the fire, or that useth divination, or an observer of times, or an enchanter, or a witch, or a charmer, or a consulter with familiar spirits, or a wizard, or a necromancer." Deuteronomy 18:10–11

> "Thou shalt not suffer a witch to live." Exodus 22:18

The core Mosaic teachings emphasise the paramountcy of loyalty to God. This is the central principle of Judaism and encapsulates monotheism, and any practise that deviates from it is forbidden. Hence why ritual magic is unlawful where it crosses the line of adulterating or denying monotheism. As such, it is regarded as anathema to the scriptures. Indeed, God is regarded as the First Principal or Cause of everything, for he is the Creator. Nonetheless, where this core doctrine is not challenged, Jewish magi down the centuries have lawfully practised rituals in God's Name. In Jewish goetia such convocations must never run contrary to the Will of God expressed in scripture or embrace idolatry. This does not rule out the practise of magic in Judaism, and never did. It simply holds it to account and lays down some ground rules for its use. Indeed, the Christian magi of the late Middle Ages were directly influenced by Jewish goetia (that is, the invocation of angels and demons).

It need not be forgotten that what also separated the authorised magic of the priesthood of both Temple and Church alike from the itinerant mage was social status.

Gnosticism

To appreciate the likely beliefs of the second century sect who claimed Simon Magus as their founder - the Simonians - we need a basic understanding of Gnosticism in the New Testament period. A feature was the rejection of sin as understood by the Church.

The Hebrew word for sin is *chet*, which means "falling short". Unlike Christianity, which later devised the doctrine of Original Sin to make sense of the state of the world, in Judaism it is held that everyone enters the world free from sin and then immediately strays from God's Law as a consequence of Adam's Fall. How this differs significantly from St. Augustine's doctrine is the moot point, but the outcome is the same: a dark barrier exists between humanity and God.

The rejection of a doctrine of sin by the Gnostics requires explanation. They were also acutely aware of the disparity of the condition of humanity from its ideal state, but chose to shift the burden of blame on to a fallen supernatural entity known as the *Demiurgos* (Demiurge or "the Half-Maker"). It was the Demiurge who created an imperfect universe, not God, nor man who ruined it. They therefore disregarded the Old Testament in its entirety, identifying the God of Israel, Yahweh, with the Demiurge. Thus, for both Jews and Christians alike, the Gnostics were regarded as being both blasphemous and licentious since their moral conduct reflected the fact they did not recognise sin or the inherent goodness of creation.

The Gnostics taught that the Demiurge had emanated from the Father God, and therefore was comprised of the same spiritous substance (*ousia*). It was from this this *prima materia* that the Demiurge created the physical universe and, with it, time and the processes of decay and death. So, let us take a step back to explain how this all came about. In Gnostic cosmogony, the Father God manifested Power and Thought within himself. These were essentially the male and female attributes of Divinity. Power and Thought engendered entities known as the Children of Light, angelic beings subject to the eternal laws, precepts, and commands of God. These beings existed within the "First Circle", which realm the Gnostics also termed "Domination". The Greek word πλήρωμα (*pleroma*, fullness or completion) is the name the Gnostics gave to Heaven. Having no distinction from God, these entities were only distinguishable between themselves by the virtues and powers they held expressed as the names given them. The collective name of these spiritual beings was αιώνας (*aeons*). These aeonic beings originally enjoyed a perfect knowledge of God's actions and powers, and were comprised of four ranks or orders, depending on the attributes they enjoyed. This was known as the "Celestial Hierarchy."

Since they were secondary beings, the aeons enjoyed inferior powers to the Father God, and plotted to limit his authority by their own thoughts and creative impulses. They hoped thereby to become creators in the Father's place. One of these aeonian beings was Sophia (Wisdom), and it was she who emanated the Demiurge from within herself. This unilateral act of creation provided the Demiurge with the material he needed to create physical life from the elements. Hence, he was the "Half-Maker", since he could not bestow immortality on the life he created. In some schools of the Secret Tradition the Demiurge is identified with Lucifer, the Light Bearer, and also with Prometheus. Due to this rebellion, God expelled the Demiurge and his followers, the Archons ("Rulers") from the Pleroma, imprisoning them in the material universe.

Christianised Gnosticism evolved a different cosmogony from its pagan counterparts. The imperfect material universe was not intended by the Father God to be a permanent prison for the fallen Archons. He desired their reconciliation and eventual reintegration with himself. Thus, the man-god Adam-Kadmon was created by God to dominate these fallen entities, with the intention of binding them and leading them back in repentance of their evil ways. Adam at this point existed as a pure spirit in a glorious disembodied form, and like the aeonian beings could read the thoughts of God (which is the meaning of his being able to "see" and "walk" with God in the Garden of Eden). Adam was given the operations (that is magic rituals) to gain command over the fallen angels through the use of their names. He was their superior. Through Adam, God conceived three distinct powers to bind the Demiurge and his demons: first, Adam was to have dominion over all passive and active life; second, Adam was granted command over nature; and third, he enjoyed command over the whole created universe and all its inhabitants. By these three operations the boundaries of power, virtue and force were innate within him. Essentially, the Demiurge was subjugated, and the process of the reintegration of the physical universe with the Father God was underway. This cosmogony explains why there is a biological interpretation of the Garden of Eden in the writings of the Simonians, because this was the place where Adam was born, and was therefore likened by them to the human womb.[14] The Gnostics believed that humanity contained a trinity of physical, psychic and spiritual parts, the latter of which was the "divine spark" or fragment of the *materia* of the Father God. They taught that this spark was innate in all people, albeit that

---

[14] Contained in the criticism of the sect written by Epiphanius of Caesarea (AD c.260–340).

some people were more advanced spiritually than others. They therefore differentiated between the "pneumatics" (spiritual people) and those who were in various stages of inferior self-knowledge.

We know from the Qumran texts that branches of Jewish mysticism – such as the Essenes - understood the universe in similarly dualistic terms. This was a world inhabited by both good and evil spirits, the invocation of whom either comprised legitimate or illegitimate magic in the eyes of mainstream Judaism. The Jewish writer Philo of Alexandria (c.20 BC – c.AD 50) wrote that while there was fluidity in the laws of nature that made magic possible, there should be a corresponding interpretation of nature with the scriptures, such that the latter's function is to define the ethical principles of its practise. (Levy, 2018)[15] According to the *Stanford Encyclopaedia of Philosophy* this approach "[was] not exclusively from the rationality of the world but by reference to a personal God who chose Israel to incarnate and bear witness to this principle in its different forms."[16] This is essentially the benchmark by which Jewish magic operated during the Second Temple period, and therein lies another principal contrast with pagan Gnosticism.

In esoteric Judaism, God created the world and everything in it as a prison to hold the fallen angels who had rebelled against him. Adam was created to restore these beings to God. Left to his free-will, Adam reflected on the power manifest in him, which led to anger and disaffected pride. The fallen angels then came to Adam in the Garden of Eden and said:

---

[15] See Lévy, Carlos, "*Philo of Alexandria*", *The Stanford Encyclopaedia of Philosophy* (Spring 2018 Edition), Edward N. Zalta (ed.) Spring 2018
[16] Ibid.

> "Did God really say, 'You must not eat from any tree in the garden?' You will certainly not die. For God knows that when you eat from it your eyes will be opened, and you will be like God, knowing good and evil."
> Genesis 3:4-5

This ill will is the principle of all spiritual evil in the Judeo-Christian tradition. By partaking of the Tree of Knowledge of Good and Evil (that is, by seeking command over all the paths of creation), Adam could no longer penetrate the will of God and hold dominion over the universe for the purpose of restoring the fallen aeons to their first estate. Consequently, the original, androgynous and incorruptible manifestation of man became incarnated (that is, born of the flesh) into its present, physical form divided by sex and subject to the forces of evolution, physical generation and death. In the words of A. E. Waite, Adam fell

> "...into the abysses of that earth whence came the fruit of his prevarication. The path of his redemption is now that of the life in Christ." (Waite, The Holy Kabballah)[17]

The apocryphal accounts of Simon Magus almost always assert that that he "boasted" of superior knowledge of the "Mind" of God through his visions. In doing so he claimed that his authority had legitimacy, and in this a parallel has been drawn with the teachings of St. Paul. From Philip the Evangelist, Simon may have come for a time to regard Jesus as the *Soter* ("Saviour") of Gnosticism, the being emanated as the Messenger of

---

[17] A.E. Waite, *The Holy Kabballah*

Light from the Father God. The first verses of the Gospel of John resonate this cosmogony

> "In the beginning was the Word, and the Word was with God, and the Word was God. The same was in the beginning with God. All things were made by him; and without him was not anything made that was made. In him was life; and the life was the light of men. And the light shineth in darkness; and the darkness comprehended it not. There was a man sent from God, whose name was John. The same came for a witness, to bear witness of the Light, that all men through him might believe. He was not that Light, but was sent to bear witness of that Light. That was the true Light, which lighteth every man that cometh into the world. He was in the world, and the world was made by him, and the world knew him not." John 1:1-10

Most New Testament scholars nowadays reject the idea these verses are remnants of a Gnostic hymn. The consensus is that the so-called "logos theology"[18] it encapsulates was more common in Hellenized Judaism than once thought, but was perhaps influenced by pagan Gnostic ideas. Equating the Mind of God with the Holy Spirit was a recurring theme of Pauline theology. The Spirit was the δύναμις (*dunamis*, power or authority) of the Godhead. In Paul's theology, it was the power of the Holy Spirit that raised Jesus to life and which reprieves all those who believe in him, both Jew and Gentile without distinction. This was a markedly different view to that of St. Peter, who at least in his early apostolic career believed that Gentile converts

---

[18] The neo-platonic doctrine of an intermediary divine being.

should become fully observant of the Jewish Law. Paul argued that Christ communicated his will on earth through the Holy Spirit, and in so doing connected the immortal spirit or spark "locked" in humanity to God's eternal Self. Through his training with Gamaliel in Jerusalem – if it happened at all - Paul would have been familiar with the Jewish doctrine of the Shekinah as an emanation or manifestation of God, concealed and revealed in everything. For Paul this was the Logos, "the Mind of Christ" for which there was no higher instructor:

> "For who hath known the mind of the Lord, that he may instruct him? but we have the mind of Christ." 1 Corinthians 2:16

Essentially the ancient world was a milieu of different cultures, concepts and ideas, and the Romanisation of the Mediterranean world expedited such exchange. Judaism - and the Primitive Church developing from it - did not exist in a cultural bubble; both encountered Graeco-Egyptian magic (Hermeticism), Gnosticism, the pagan Mystery cults and a whole raft of other philosophical influences. Therefore, whether Simon Magus was an allegorised "type" of heretic or an historical individual, it can be said that he existed, and his confrontation with the Church in Jerusalem tells us a good deal about the world of magic and miracles he inhabited.

M.R. Osborne, M.A.
Northampton, June 2022

1. Shim`on of Gitta

> "In the last days the mountain of the Lord's Temple will be established as chief among the mountains; it will be raised above the hills, and peoples will stream to it."
> Micah 4:1

Simon (Shim`on in Aramaic) is said to have originated from the Samarian town of Gitta, now the Palestinian village of Jit in the West Bank. Modern Jit is the home of two and a half thousand people, much less than its ancient, almost entirely Samaritan, population. The village is some six miles west of Nablus, not far from the ancient quarries cut into the porous limestone peaks of Mounts Gerizim and Ebal. The terrain is hot and rugged. Agriculture is still the principle economy of the area and which continues under pressure from Israel, in the form of restricted water supplies from the diverted natural aquifers supplying the encroaching Israeli settlements. An interesting insight into Simon's background is found in the detail contained in the Pseudo-Clementine account of his childhood:

> " ... once when my mother Rachel ordered me to go to the field to reap, and I saw a sickle lying, I ordered it to go and reap; and it reaped ten times more than the others. Lately, I produced many new sprouts from the earth, and made them bear leaves and produce fruit in a moment; and the nearest mountain I successfully bored through."[19]

---

[19] See Ante-Nicene Fathers, Vol VIII: Pseudo-Clementine Literature: Chapter IX (sacred-texts.com)

In ancient times, Josephus[20] wrote of Samaria:

> " ... as to the country of Samaria, it lies between Judea and Galilee; it begins at a village that is in the great plain called Ginea, and ends at the Acrabbene toparchy, and is entirely of the same nature with Judea; for both countries are made up of hills and valleys, and are moist enough for agriculture, and are very fruitful. They have abundance of trees, and are full of autumnal fruit, both that which grows wild, and that which is the effect of cultivation. They are not naturally watered by many rivers, but derive their chief moisture from rain-water, of which they have no want; and for those rivers which they have, all their waters are exceeding sweet: by reason also of the excellent grass they have, their cattle yield more milk than do those in other places; and, what is the greatest sign of excellency and of abundance, they each of them are very full of people." ((trans.))[21] Josephus, *The Jewish War*

The Samaritans

The name of the region is derived from the city of the same name, the former capital of the Kingdom of Israel (930 BC – 720 BC). The Samaritans broke away from Judaism when the prophet Eli abandoned the Temple established by God on Mount Gerizim to establish a

---

[20] Josephus Flavius (AD c.37-c.93)
[21] Josephus Flavius : *The Jewish War*. III.3, trans. William Whiston. Complete works of Josephus online at http://ccel.wheaton.edu/j/josephus

rival sanctuary at Shiloh.[22] This event ushered in what the Samaritans still refer to as "the Era of Divine Disfavour" when God turned away from the Jewish people.

In not following Eli to Shiloh, those clinging to the Gerizim Temple regarded themselves as the "Chosen Ones" remaining faithful to God. This schism occurred during the second century BC, and the Samaritan faith retained many features in common with Judaism. Both faith systems venerated the Torah (the first five books of the Bible). This distinguishing attachment to Mount Gerazim took on greater significance following the destruction of the Jerusalem Temple by the emperor Titus in AD 70. Whereas the Rabbinate filled the void left by the redundant Jerusalem Temple priesthood, the Samaritans continued in the observance of sacerdotal worship on their holy mountain.

In the New Testament book of Acts, Simon is active in the nearby city and environs of Samaria. The epithet ὁ μάγος ("the Magus") does not appear in the New Testament, where he is instead described as μαγεύων, *mageuōn*a ("the sorcerer").[23] The term "magus" was used disparagingly by the later Christians, despite magic being a legitimate part of Jewish culture at that time. Indeed, there was probably nothing of a derogatory nature intended in the designation "a practitioner of magic."

The title "Magus" when applied to Simon occurs in the later post-apostolic writings. The second century Christian apologist Justin Martyr (AD c.100 – c.165) who originated from Flavia Neapolis (Shechem) in Samaria, wrote that "many" Samarians were followers

---

[22] This was during the period of the Judges (1367-1050 BC).
[23] Acts 8:9

of Simon of Gitta.[24] These he dubbed "Simonians". Epiphanius (c.AD 310-320-c.403) bishop of Constantia in Cyprus, wrote that:

> "Simon was a sorcerer, and came from Gitthon, the city in Samaria – though it is a village now. He deluded the Samarian people by deceiving and catching them with his feats of magic and said that he was the supreme power of God and had come down from on high. To Samaritans he called himself the Father; but to Jews he said he was the Son, though he had suffered without suffering, but suffered only in appearance." [25]

In the Pseudo-Clementine literature[26] of the third to fourth centuries AD, we discover that Simon declined to establish his sect in Jerusalem, and insisted on forming it at Mount Gerizim, which whispers of vestiges of a credible Samaritan provenance. If so, there is less reason to doubt Justin Martyr's earlier testimony concerning him. In the Acts of Peter there is a further hint of Simon's Samaritan origins:

> "And on the following day Simon the magician, and Peter and Paul the Apostles of Christ, came into Nero, and Simon said: "These are the disciples of the Nazarene, and it is not at all well that they should have the protection of the Jews." Nero said: "What is a Nazarene?" Simon said: "There is a city of Judah which has always been opposed to us, called Nazareth, and to it

---

[24] First Apology, xxvi
[25] Ibid. Epiphanius 2,1
[26] So named because of the claimed authorship of the text by St. Clement, bishop of Rome (died between AD c.100-c.110).

> the teacher of these men belonged." Acts of Peter 16

If we consider the intensely cosmopolitan Mediterranean world of the first century, we should not be surprised by the almost febrile desire of the primitive Church to identify itself as authentically Jewish. Neither must we forget that Simon was probably not a Jew. Peter's confrontation with Simon in the Book of Acts would therefore be a characteristically brutal and sharp encounter with grievances running between Jew and Samaritan that ran far deeper than a disagreement over simony. The Lucan account describes Simon as being terrified of Peter and repentant at his recalcitrance:

> "Then answered Simon, and said, 'Pray ye to the Lord for me, that none of these things which ye have spoken come upon me.'" Acts 8:24

Contrary to this perspective of him, Simon appears to have found a popular following in Samaria. Not only in Justin Martyr, but also in the Pseudo-Clementine *Recognitions and Homilies*, we read accounts describing the sect claiming him as their founder. The passage of time may cast doubt on the reliability of these latter testimonies, yet they probably contain elements of historical fact:

> "This Simon's father was Antonius, and his mother Rachel. By nation he is a Samaritan, from a village of the Gettones; by profession a magician yet exceedingly well trained in the Greek literature."[27]

---

[27] Op. Cit. Ante-Nicene Fathers, Vol VIII: *Pseudo-Clementine Literature* Chapter VII (sacred-texts.com)

What is surprising is the identity of Simon's parents being mentioned at all. The above passage from Pseudo-Clement states that he was "exceedingly well educated", suggestive perhaps that he came from a prosperous background. The *Jewish Encyclopaedia* refers to the mention of Simon in the early Christian Clementine *Recognitiones* as follows:

> "[These texts] … represent Simon as a Jewish magician instead of a Samaritan, stating that he was a member of a Jewish household in Caesarea, and that, when pursued by Peter, he fled to Judea. Mention is made, moreover, of a magician named Simon who lived in this very city of Caesarea about the year 40 of the common era (Josephus, Ant. xx. 7, 2); so that some scholars consider the two to be identical." (Kohler)[28]

The Practitioner of Magic

Luke's description of Simon's self-styled designation as "the greatest" hints that he enjoyed an inherent natural ability in sorcery. To develop any innate skill, the adept of the ancient world was generally required to be educated and well trained. Otherwise, such abilities were generally regarded as limited to minor powers. The practice of itinerant magic was very common in the first century, and if Simon hailed from a Hellenised family (as the sources suggest), he may have been a professional sorcerer. Hans Diete-Betz in his *Introduction to the Greek Magical Papyri*, states that the "wandering mage" was a familiar element in the culture of the time:

---

[28] See JewishEncyclopedia.com

"There are texts reflecting perhaps a different type of magician, a type we know from the Greek religious milieu. This type of wandering craftsman seems keen to adopt and adapt every religious tradition that appeared useful to him, while the knowledge and understanding of what he adopted was characterized by a certain superficiality. This type of magician no longer understood the old languages, although he used remnants of them in transcription. He recited and used what must at one time have been metrically composed hymns; but he no longer recognized the meter, and he spoiled it when he inserted his own material. In the hands of magicians of this type, the gods from the various cults gradually merged, and as their natures became blurred, they often changed into completely different deities. For these magicians, there was no longer any cultural difference between the Egyptian and the Greek gods, or between them and the Jewish god and the Jewish angels; and even Jesus was occasionally assimilated into this truly "ecumenical" religious syncretism of the Hellenistic world culture."[29]

The ritualised control of nature through the evocation of spirits may have resembled the following medieval grimoire, which in turn owed its antecedence to an older tradition, bearing witness to the magical papyri destroyed during the censorship purge in the reign of the emperor Tiberius:[30]

---

[29] Hans Diete-Betz, *Introduction to the Greek Magical Papyri*, p.46
[30] Possibly alluded to in the burning of the magic scrolls in Acts 19.

> "I conjure thee by Him to Whom all creatures are obedient, by this ineffable Name TETRAGRAMMATON JEHOVAH, by which the elements are overthrown, the air is shaken, the sea turns back, the fire is generated, the earth moves and all the hosts of things celestial, of things terrestrial, of things infernal, do tremble and are confounded together."[31]

Josephus refers to Simon as "a sorcerer" in his *Antiquities of the Jews*:

> "While Felix was procurator of Judea, he saw this Drusilla, and fell in love with her; for she did indeed exceed all other women in beauty; and he sent to her a person whose name was Simon, one of his friends; a Jew he was, and by birth a Cypriot, and one who pretended to be a magician, and endeavoured to persuade her to forsake her present husband, and marry him; and promised, that if she would not refuse him, he would make her a happy woman."[32]

This is a passage which will bear significance later, when we discuss the lurid descriptions of Simon's female consort Helena (in the sources sometimes called Helen). By tradition, Helena was a slave girl whom Simon rescued from enforced prostitution in Antioch and who became his partner and counterpart. Helena appears in the pseudepigraphal accounts of Simon's encounters with the Apostles Peter and Paul.

The fledgling Church sought to stabilise its position in Samaria (Acts 8:25). Yet why did Saints Peter and James return to Jerusalem so quickly? Is this

---

[31] Ceremonial magic p.241
[32] Josephus, *Antiquities of the Jews,* Book XX, Ch.7:2

another instance of Luke smoothing over the cracks in the historical record? In Acts 8:26 we read that Philip the Evangelist left Samaria "soon afterwards", and it is beginning to feel as if the Apostles came up from Jerusalem to tackle Simon because Philip needed their help, but were unable to make any meaningful headway against him either. Therefore the Book of Acts may be intentionally down-playing what happened:

> "And the angel of the Lord spake unto Philip, saying, 'Arise, and go toward the south unto the way that goeth down from Jerusalem unto Gaza, which is desert.'" Acts 8:26

Which is all very convenient; as is the fact that Simon Magus is not mentioned again in the New Testament. Philip's subsequent self-imposed removal to the desert around Gaza implies that he needed to exorcise himself from whatever he encountered in Samaria. Ritualised cleansing in the desert was a practise mandated by the Temple priesthood itself, as we shall see when we discuss the scapegoat of Yom Kippur. The situation 'on the ground' therefore appears to reenforce Justin Martyr's description of Samaria as a hotbed of Simonianism after all.

Yet we need to understand the motivation of the Primitive Church in seeking out Simon in the first place, because this informs the entire debate. Hans von Campenausen addressed this issue in his seminal work *Ecclesiastical Authority and Spiritual Power in the Church of the First Three Centuries*:

> "For the primitive community Jesus *had* risen; and with this sign of the imminent consummation of the age a twofold reality had become a certainty for their faith. On the one hand, the riddle of his person is now resolved by

God himself; Jesus is the living Lord and Redeemer, Messiah and Son of Man, soon to return on the clouds of heaven. On the other, the revelation of this truth simultaneously brought with it the conviction that the gathering and renewal of Israel, the eschatological people of God, must now begin. In Jewish expectation the one could not be separated from the other; and the enthusiastic spirit of holiness, which in fulfilment of the ancient prophecies was poured out on all who believed in and were baptised into the Name of Jesus, made the realisation of the promise a matter of direct experience." (Campenhausen, 1969, pp. 12-13)

The Book of Acts recollects this expectation in its description of the activities of the first generation of Christian missionaries in Samaria, although by the time of its composition at the end of the first century the events it described were already outside living memory and were being reinterpreted to suit its agenda. Nonetheless, the implication is that the followers of Simon were active in Samaria at the time, because it would have been much easier for Luke not to have mentioned the Magus at all. If so, it may with some degree of confidence be said that the historical Simon came to reject the authority and teachings of the Apostolic Church.

For the Samaritans, the equivalent of the Messiah was the Taheb ("Restorer"). The Taheb was expected to restore the ancient rights and privileges of the Samaritans and, like the Jewish *Mashiach* (Messiah) would revive the Kingdom of Israel. However, the Taheb would also restore the Temple at Mount Gerizim. He was expected to have been born a Samaritan, not a Jew, and his appearance would coincide with "the Day of the Lord" i.e. God's judgement and not as an augur of a future second advent as taught by the Christians.

It may be fair to surmise that Philip's mission to Samaria was aimed at proselytising the local Jewish minority, avoiding the Samaritan population. If there was a breakdown in relations between Philip and Simon then it may have been inspired by differences in eschatological expectation. This in turn, reflects an even deeper issue facing the two groups, since Jesus' selection of Twelve disciples - of whom Peter and John were prominent - was essentially a statement of authority:

> "The Twelve were formed in view of the coming kingdom of God, and they enter on their real duties only at the Last Day, when they are to sit on twelve thrones, judging the twelve tribes of Israel. It is in in expectation of this hour, which is to exalt them to the supreme honour, that they regard it as their prime duty not to depart from Jerusalem."[33]

Little wonder that Simon and Peter clashed so dramatically. Indeed, according to the unanimous report of the post-apostolic era writers such as Justin Martyr, Simon appears to have persisted in his distinct views, whatever those were. The writers of the early Church therefore came to present him as the first heretic, the "Father of Heresies".

The Father of Heresies

The Book of Acts and Justin Martyr's *First Apology* smooth over discord in the Primitive Church as it migrated into broader Hellenic culture. These writings nevertheless preserve critical parts of a carefully

---

[33] Ibid. p.16

preserved oral tradition concerning the Apostolate which is most informative. The earliest Christians believed in Jesus as the fulfilment of scripture *in person*, and in the immanency of his Second Coming. This is why so little was written down about him during that critical period; there was no point because Christ's return on clouds of glory was set to occur during the lifetime of the Twelve. It was only when the Apostles were dying that written accounts began to be circulated in order to preserve their teachings. Indeed, if we consider the epic Greek poem The *Iliad*, we can appreciate the strength of unwritten transmission in antiquity. Homer's *Illiad* is understood to be extant, and what is truly incredible is that the poem and characters in it were known *centuries* after its oral composition before it was finally written down.

The longevity of oral tradition is an aspect almost entirely ignored by Hermann Detering in his book *The Falsified Paul: Early Christianity in the Twilight* (Journal of Higher Criticism).[34] In it, Detering attacks the historicity and validity of the entire Pauline corpus, using outdated redactionist criticism to argue the material was either written too late or else by Gnostic factions within the early Church. He argues this to the point where the historical person of St. Paul never existed. These ideas are not new. Rudolph Bultmann wrote extensively on the allegorical and existentialist value of the New Testament, to such an extent that historical analysis was regarded as utterly futile. Even the epistles generally attributed to Paul by scholarship are refuted by Detering, with the Apostle reduced to a Gnostic invention.

Why is this relevant? Because some scholars have argued that St. Paul is none other than Simon Magus. If Paul existed - and even Detering suggests

---

[34] Journal of Higher Criticism (2003)

Justin Martyr was familiar with the Apostle's written style - then he may have been a Gnostic heretic.[35] For Detering:

> " ... this can finally be explained, however, only when we interrogate our last and decisive witness, Marcion, the 'rediscoverer' of the Pauline letters who was excommunicated from the Catholic church." (Detering, p. 71).

He adds:

> "It became more and more clear to me that anyone who would base his historical knowledge of the Apostle on Acts must tumble into the deep, golden abyss of fairy tales and legends. Historical certainty could never be found here. The question whether anything at all in the presentation of Acts could have historical value could basically not be answered by a historian who was aware of his responsibility. If one did not want to simply dismiss everything as unhistorical (one really could not blame someone who reached such a radical conclusion), all that remains is the simple statement that we have to do here with an Apostle, who presumably worked around the middle of the first century, who was an important missionary, and who may have died in Rome."[36]

The problem with this argument is that it ignores the accuracy of oral transmission at that time. It also misses the point that Acts and the broader corpus of New

---

[35] After Marcion of Sinope (AD c.110-160)
[36] Ibid. p.24

Testament literature deliberately papers over the cracks of an early schism between Peter and Paul. In short, one has to read between the lines of the earliest sources, a little like picking up a popular sensationalist tabloid and scanning it for any real news. An instance of this occurs when Detering considers Paul's opposition to ritual circumcision, likening this to a Marcionite doctrine.[37]

If we accept a likely composition date of around AD 90 - 110 for the Book of Acts, then it places the source material firmly within second or third generation testimony. It is a little like recalling your grandfather's war stories relayed through your parents; they are true but the details are missing. The problem is not so much with the dating of the Lucan narratives, but with the agenda of the Christian sect in its circumambulation around the Graeco-Roman world. For instance, Detering makes much of the apparent dichotomy between the description of Paul's visit to Jerusalem immediately after his conversion as recounted in Acts, and that in Galatians where he went "to Arabia" instead.[38] Clearly we must take the older, primary sources at face value, and assume Paul existed, but that is not really the issue. It is blatantly obvious that he went to Jerusalem to meet or debate with the Apostles at some point (which the authentic Pauline letters attest). In any event, the region called Arabia in Galatians was the Roman province of Arabia Petrea, with its capital at Petra. It lay within a mere week's travel from Jerusalem. Furthermore, Paul had no less than four visits to Jerusalem recorded in the New Testament. The first is described in Galatians 1:18-24 and Acts 9:26-30. A subsequent trip is mentioned in Acts 11:28-30; a third is described in Galatians 2:1-

---

[37] So named after Marcion of Sinope (AD c. 85 – 160) a Christian Gnostic writer.

[38] Galatians 1:15–17

10 and Acts 15. A final trip is recorded in Romans 15:25-28, 1 Corinthians 16:1-4 and Acts 21:15-18. It is likely therefore that in this impressive corpus of contemporary and near-contemporary material, that Paul both existed and visited the Church at Jerusalem. Paul even affirms that Peter had the special charge of being Apostle to the Jews, just as he, Paul, was "Apostle to the Gentiles":

> "For he that wrought effectually in Peter to the Apostleship of the circumcision, the same was mighty in me toward the Gentiles." Galatians 2:8

It is therefore improbable that Simon Magus and St. Paul were the same man, albeit both had certain commonalities: both appear to have been well educated and were from Hellenised Semitic backgrounds. Yet, if Simon was a Samaritan, then he is unlikely to have accepted the core Pauline doctrine of salvation apart from the Law, any more than he would accept a messiah from the 'heretic' Jews who refused to worship on Mount Gerizim. That said, if Simon abandoned Samaritanism (which as we shall see is likely), then these stumbling blocks would no longer compel any such divergence of views.

We get the impression from his description in the Book of Acts that Simon was a larger-than-life character, who was "taking over" the milder Philip's mission in Samaria. There are certainly shades of Pauline theology manifesting in the Lucan account, in the form of a hint that Simon interpreted Philip's baptism as a purificatory washing. This is something that Paul would never have accepted. We will look at Simon's baptism in more detail later, but the Christian version of baptism differed markedly from traditional Jewish cleansing ceremonies, and this may explain why

Peter and John were sent to help Philip deal with Simon:

> "But when they believed Philip preaching the things concerning the kingdom of God, and the name of Jesus Christ, they were baptized, both men and women ... Now when the Apostles which were at Jerusalem heard that Samaria had received the word of God, they sent unto them Peter and John: who, when they were come down, prayed for them, that they might receive the Holy Ghost: (for as yet he was fallen upon none of them: only they were baptized in the name of the Lord Jesus.)" Acts 8:12,14-16

2. Shimon of Bethsaida

Finding the St. Peter of history is even more difficult than discovering the elusive Shim'on of Gitta. Aside from the disputed rediscovery of his Vatican tomb, there are five primary sources by which we may attempt a reconstruction of the life of the saint known to his contemporaries as Shim'on of Bethsaida. These are:

- the Synoptic Gospels and the Book of Acts;
- the Gospel of John and the remaining Johannine sources;
- the corpus of Pauline material; and
- apocryphal literature, such as the Acts of Peter.

According to the Gospel of John, the fishing village of Bethsaida on the northern shore of the Sea of Galilee was Peter's home.[39] Bethsaida is most likely the abandoned settlement el-Araj, which now lies approximately one and a half miles inland from the shoreline (Nun, 1998).[40] The Synoptic Gospels recount that Peter's mother-in-law lived in Capernaum.[41] His extended family may therefore have lived in Jesus' village, and we are told that Peter owned a boat and was a fisherman.[42] In the Acts of Peter he is said to have had a disabled daughter. As with Simon Magus, Peter's original name was Shim'on (prior to his renaming by Jesus as Cephas, Aramaic for Petros, meaning "the Rock").

---

[39] John 1:44
[40] https://www.jerusalemperspective.com/905/
[41] Matthew 8:14–17, Mark 1:29–31, Luke 4:38. 1 Corinthians 9:5 has also been taken to imply that Peter was married.
[42] Luke 5:3

Acts describes Peter's dream, whereby he receives a vision from God permitting the consumption of food prohibited by the Law. The passage is a Lucan attempt to reconcile the Jewish and Gentile dispute in the early Church and, indeed, from that point Peter becomes a leading proponent for the evangelisation of the Gentiles without having to follow the Law (Acts 9:32–10:2). These accounts stand in contrast to the likely views of the historic Peter, at least in his early ministry. It is probable that he believed that the Gentiles were to be saved by incorporation into Israel, not separately from it. This would have applied to Samaritan converts as well. Hence Peter's words in Acts are unlikely to have been spoken by the Apostle:

> "Then Peter opened his mouth, and said, 'Of a truth I perceive that God is no respecter of persons: But in every nation he that feareth him, and worketh righteousness, is accepted with him. The word which God sent unto the children of Israel, preaching peace by Jesus Christ: (he is Lord of all). That word, I say, ye know, which was published throughout all Judaea, and began from Galilee, after the baptism which John preached.'" Acts 10:34-37

The interesting point about the above passage is that there are discernible fragments of historical accuracy regarding Peter's early ministry. These are:

- that Peter's ministry was in Judea (not in Rome or anywhere else); and
- he was familiar with the teachings of John the Baptist.

In Acts 8:14 Peter and the Apostle John depart Jerusalem for Samaria at Philip's request. One cannot come to any other conclusion other than Philip was struggling to assert his authority there, and specifically that he was unable to manage Simon Magus, whose "greatness" it appears had attracted a significant local following.

The ruins of Caesarea, nineteenth century Bible illustration

Prison Break

Tellingly, there is not one word contained in Acts about Peter's rejection of Simon's sorcery. This suggests the Apostles were not unduly concerned about magic, but *were* concerned about Simon Magus' intentions. Were they worried about the response from the locals if they appeared weak? That Peter is unconcerned about Simon's magic tells us that he was familiar with its commonplace practice, and that he did not necessarily regard it as unlawful, otherwise we can be sure of its mention in his chastisement of Simon. In fact, in Acts 12:3-19 Peter is miraculously freed from gaol by an angel after his incarceration by king Agrippa.[43] There is a

---

[43] Acts 12. Agrippa I (10 BC – AD 44). Agrippa was the grandson of Herod the Great and son of Aristobulus IV, the last king of Judea.

similar instance, again in Acts, when Paul and Silas are "praying and singing hymns" at midnight when they are freed from prison by supernatural forces.[44] Might such instances be indicative of the use of evocation by the Primitive Church for angelic help? Might this be an example of the weaving together of magical forces to influence a beneficial outcome? We can, alas, do little more than read between the lines.

However he managed it, after his liberation Peter departed Jerusalem to go to "another place", most likely Antioch in Asia Minor[45] (modern-day Antakya, in Turkey). Here, according to Galatians 2:11, Paul opposed him "to his face, because he [Peter] was in the wrong." This incident is similar to the confrontation between Peter and Simon Magus in Acts and that mentioned in the apocryphal Acts of Peter (the latter of which also took place in Antioch). Coincidence? Acts 8 describes Peter as full of indignation when he sharply rebukes Simon:

> "And when Simon saw that through laying on of the Apostles' hands the Holy Ghost was given, he offered them money, saying, 'Give me also this power, that on whomsoever I lay hands, he may receive the Holy Ghost.' But Peter said unto him, 'Thy money perish with thee, because thou hast thought that the gift of God may be purchased with money. Thou hast neither part nor lot in this matter: for thy heart is not right in the sight of God. Repent therefore of this thy wickedness, and pray God, if perhaps the thought of thine heart may be forgiven thee. For

---

[44] Acts 16:25-26
[45] According to Origen and Eusebius in his Church History (III, 36) Peter had founded the church of Antioch.

I perceive that thou art in the gall of bitterness, and in the bond of iniquity.'" Acts 8:18-23

Harsh words indeed, and which are reflected in the apocryphal Peter accusing Simon of manipulating and stealing from a wealthy woman in Judea. If there remain any historical vestiges in these confrontations, then they appear to have become highly personal. In the Acts of Peter, Simon's words are as terse as those of the saint:

> "I wonder, O good emperor, that you reckon this man of any consequence—a man uneducated, a fisherman of the poorest, and endowed with power neither in word nor by rank." Acts of Peter 18

Peter tackled the threat in Samaria face-on, in much the same way as he had dealt with his differences with Paul. In that sense, much of his contest with Simon has a ring of truth about it. Yet, we seem to return time and again to curious similarities between Simon Magus and St. Paul. If we consider for a moment the key theological differences between Peter and Paul in the New Testament, we quickly detect a serious divergence of views between the two men over the continuance of Jewish purificatory laws, which in turn becomes a power contest which some suggest indicates that Paul might have been Simon Magus. Thus, for instance, in contrast to Paul, in Acts 2:16-17 and 3:21,24-26 we read that Peter believed the Jews remained the designated Chosen People through whom prophecy was to be fulfilled. In Matthew[46], Luke[47] and Acts,[48] the Gentiles are blessed

---

[46] Matthew 10:5
[47] Luke 24:49
[48] Acts 11:19

through Israel, God's earthly representation.[49] In 1 Peter[50] there is a promise of an earthly inheritance, which is very much in keeping with the traditional Jewish concept of Messianic redemption:

> "But ye are a chosen generation, a royal priesthood, an holy nation, a peculiar people; that ye should shew forth the praises of him who hath called you out of darkness into his marvellous light." 1 Peter 2:9

However, for Paul there is an ethereal, heavenly salvation in another body and another world altogether,[51] one which feels very Gnostic in its overtones. Peter regarded salvation as "of the Jews" led by the twelve heads of the tribes of Israel sitting in judgement at the forthcoming Second Advent[52] of Jesus.[53] In contrast, Paul describes a tough confrontation with Peter and the Twelve in Jerusalem:

> "But contrariwise, when they saw that the gospel of the uncircumcision was committed unto me, as the gospel of the circumcision was unto Peter (for he that wrought effectually in Peter to the Apostleship of the circumcision, the same was mighty in me toward the Gentiles. And when James, Cephas, and John, who seemed to be pillars, perceived the grace that was given unto

---

[49] As we read in Isaiah, Revelation and 1 Peter
[50] 1 Peter 1:4
[51] Philippians 3:20, Ephesians 2:6 and 1 Thessalonians 4:17
[52] John 4:22, Matthew 19:28, 1 Peter 1:10 and Revelation 21:14
[53] James 2:24, 1 John 2:5, Matthew 19:27 and Hebrews 10:26

> me, they gave to me and Barnabas the right hands of fellowship; that we should go unto the heathen, and they unto the circumcision. Only they would that we should remember the poor; the same which I also was forward to do. But when Peter was come to Antioch, I withstood him to the face, because he was to be blamed."
> Galatians 2:7-11

An interesting parallel occurs in the Clementine literature of the third and fourth centuries. Here we read of the legend of Peter making his way from Judea to Antioch, where he encounters Simon Magus. The story goes that the debate lasted three days. In the Acts of Peter and in Eusebius of Caesarea (c.AD 260–c.340) it is stated that Simon fled to Rome following Peter's rebuke in Samaria. Does this not remind us of Paul's appeal to Festus to escape the inquisition of the Jerusalem Sanhedrin?

> "Then the High Priest and the chief of the Jews informed him against Paul, and besought him, and desired favour against him, that he would send for him to Jerusalem, laying wait in the way to kill him. But Festus answered, that Paul should be kept at Caesarea, and that he himself would depart shortly thither. Let them therefore, said he, which among you are able, go down with me, and accuse this man, if there be any wickedness in him. And when he had tarried among them more than ten days, he went down unto Caesarea; and the next day sitting on the judgment seat commanded Paul to be brought. And when he was come, the Jews which came down from Jerusalem stood round about and laid many and grievous complaints against Paul, which they could not prove. While he answered

for himself, Neither against the law of the Jews, neither against the temple, nor yet against Caesar, have I offended anything at all. But Festus, willing to do the Jews a pleasure, answered Paul, and said, Wilt thou go up to Jerusalem, and there be judged of these things before me? Then said Paul, I stand at Caesar's judgment seat, where I ought to be judged: to the Jews have I done no wrong, as thou very well knowest. For if I be an offender, or have committed any thing worthy of death, I refuse not to die but if there be none of these things whereof these accuse me, no man may deliver me unto them. I appeal unto Caesar. ^{12}Then Festus, when he had conferred with the council, answered, Hast thou appealed unto Caesar? unto Caesar shalt thou go." Acts 25:2-12

There is something a little awry in the similarities of these stories, but in all probably they are merely coincidental.

The Rock

Something of the robust, fiery character of Peter pervades the New Testament narratives. In the Gospel of Luke, Peter is the first of the disciples to investigate Jesus' tomb when he sprints to it. Luke also records Christ's exclamation: "Simon, Simon, behold, Satan hath desired to have you, that he may sift you as wheat: but I have prayed for thee, that thy faith fail not: and when thou art converted, strengthen thy brethren."[54] John states that it was Peter who cut off Malchus' ear with a sword in the Garden of Gethsemane.[55] Actions that

---

[54] Luke 22:31
[55] John 18:10

made Peter the strong man, the Rock, the alpha-male and foundation stone of the Church. He appears to lack neither leadership skills nor courage:

> "And I tell you that you are Cephas, and on this stone I will build my Church, and the gates of Hades will not overcome it. I will give you the keys of the kingdom of heaven; whatever you bind on earth will be bound in heaven, and whatever you loose on earth will be loosed in heaven." Matthew 16:18

If we wish to consider Peter's view of magic, we need look no further than the miracle stories of Jesus' earthly ministry. The miracle of the saint walking on water is an event that is, surprisingly, described in the Gospel of John as well as in the Synoptic Gospels of Matthew and Mark. In the Gospel of Matthew, Peter briefly walks on water before sinking when his heart is no longer "right" in the sight of God.[56] We will return to the magic of transvection (flight) later, but there is a similarity between walking on water levitation in the air. Both demonstrate the power of domination over the elements.

One cannot help but smile at the similarity of Peter's character exposé of Simon Magus as an "angry man" of wavering faith. The most telling connection is that Peter's brother Andrew,[57] was one of at least two of the twelve Apostles who had once been disciples of John the Baptist. Simon may have accepted Philip the Evangelist's mission, at least initially, because of this

---

[56] Matthew 14:28–31
[57] From the Hebrew נדר (*nadar*), "to vow" and דרר (*darar*)," to flow freel", suggestive perhaps this was an initiatory name given to Andrew by John the Baptist.

connection. There was also an apparent link between Peter's close family and John the Baptist[58] and, if Simon Magus had been a disciple of John, then the two men might conceivably have been acquainted (or at least known of one another). If so, Acts brushes out of history Peter's prior knowledge of Simon, just as it does the bristling confrontation between Peter and Paul.[59] Instead, Peter's powers (or authority) are juxtaposed with Simon's "greatness" to address the question of legitimacy.

Yet what is prayer if not invocation? In English, the noun "invocation" is a spoken word, or set of words, designed to *invite the Presence of God*. According to *The Catholic Encyclopaedia*:

> "In hearing our prayer God does not change His will or action in our regard, but simply puts into effect what He had eternally decreed in view of our prayer. This He may do directly without the intervention of any secondary cause as when He imparts to us some supernatural gift, such as actual grace, or indirectly, when He bestows some natural gift. In this latter case He directs by His Providence the natural causes which contribute to the effect desired, whether they be moral or free agents, such as men; or some moral and others not, but physical and not free; or, when none of them is free. Finally, by miraculous intervention, and without employing any of these causes, He can produce the effect prayed for." (Catholic Encyclopedia)[60]

---

[58] John 1:35-36

[59] **Galatians 2:11:** "But when Peter was come to Antioch, I withstood him to the face, because he was to be blamed."

[60] See newadvent.org

Therefore – and to emphasise the point - the difference in legitimacy lays in the petitioner's *intentions* coalescing with the settled will of God. This does not differ in any material way from the view of first century Judaism concerning the right or wrong use of magic, and reflects Peter's words in his rebuke of Simon Magus that he is being denied the gifts of the Holy Spirit because he is emotionally unprepared, disagreeable, and not acting with the right intentions. It would seem to have nothing to do with simony. In the Acts of Peter, the Apostle's focus is very much on Simon's false teachings, deceit, and antagonism towards the authority of the Church:

> "And Peter said, "O good emperor. This Simon is full of lies and deceit, even if it should seem that he is what he is not—a god. And in Christ there is all excellent victory through God and through man. But in this Simon, there are two essences, of man and of devil, who through man endeavours to ensnare men." … Nero said: Are you not afraid, Peter, of Simon, who confirms his godhead by deeds?" Peter said: "Godhead is in Him who searches the hidden things of the heart." Acts of Peter 17,19

Simon Magus is portrayed as a practitioner of almost exemplary magical powers because, of course, the Church could not deny them. Simon's nefarious intentions are frustrated by Peter when he attempts to fully utilise them for his own benefit. Peter makes no comment in Acts 8 about Simon's sorcery, but instead directs the following personal criticism at him:

i. dishonesty ("Thy money perish with thee, because thou hast thought that the gift of God may be purchased with money");

ii.   narcissism ("Thou hast neither part nor lot in this matter"); and

iii.   lack of right intention ("Thy heart is not right in the sight of God"; "Pray that the thought of thine heart may be forgiven thee"; and "I perceive that thou art in the gall of bitterness and in the bond of iniquity."

3. Charism

According to the Gospel of Luke, Simon Magus offered the Apostles money in exchange for the imposition of hands bestowing the powers of the Holy Spirit upon him:

> "And when Simon saw that through laying on of the Apostles' hands the Holy Ghost was given, he offered them money, saying, Give me also this power, that on whomsoever I lay hands, he may receive the Holy Ghost." Acts 8:18-19

Simon's blatant request (from whence the English term "simony" arose[61]) elicits an extremely negative response from the Church. To understand why, we need to consider the importance of the laying on of hands practiced by the Temple priests in the transmission of sacramental charisms (such as healing and blessing).

> "And he shall put his hand upon the head of the burnt offering; and it shall be accepted for him to make atonement for him. And he shall kill the bullock before the Lord: and the priests, Aaron's sons, shall bring the blood, and sprinkle the blood round about upon the altar that is by the door of the tabernacle of the congregation." Leviticus 1:4-5

---

[61] The act of simony, or paying for position, is named after Simon who tried to buy his way into the power of the Apostles.

The Day of Atonement

Yom Kippur (the Day of Atonement) is a period of purificatory abstinence in Judaism. In the Temple period the High Priests were presented with two goats destined to die in atonement for Israel's sins. The High Priest laid both of his hands upon the first goat in order to transfer the sin upon it, and sacrificed the animal before destroying its physical form in a fire. He placed his hands on the head of the second goat before sending the animal into the desert with a man who pushed it to its death from a cliff. This latter was the scapegoat *sa'ir la-'Azae'zel* ("goat for Azaezal"). The man who pushed the goat off the precipice remained unclean - and vulnerable to psychic attack by Azaezal - for forty days. He had to ritually cleanse himself in the Judean Desert for that period of time, symbolically taking on the role of the Hebrews' wanderings through Sinai.

Azaezel was a fallen angel, one of the aeons cast from Heaven and imprisoned in the physical universe. He was said to occupy the wilderness, and it was he who prompted the Hebrews to complain about the lack of provisions during their forty-year plight. It is likely to have been Azaezal that Jesus encountered when he fasted for forty days and nights during his ritual purification following his baptism by John. The demon also appears in the esoteric literature at Qumran.[62] In 1 Enoch he is identified with murder, destruction and lamentation:

> "Azaezal, thou shalt have no peace: a severe sentence has gone forth against thee to put thee in bonds: and thou shalt not have toleration nor

---

[62] Azazel occurs in the line 6 of 4Q203, *The Book of Giants*, which is a part of the Enochian literature found at Qumran.

request granted to thee, because of the unrighteousness which thou hast taught, and because of all the works of godlessness and unrighteousness and sin which thou hast shown to men." 1 Enoch 13:1-2

For the Church, the shedding of Christ's blood made the continuance of sacrifice unnecessary, since the Messiah as the Lamb of God had taken on the sin of the world instead. His resurrection signified the reunion of body, mind and soul as a mirror image of man's original glorified state. Blood sacrifices were therefore no longer required, except in its symbolic repetition in the Eucharist. Yet the imposition of hands continued, and not only in a symbolic manner, as recalled by St. Paul when he met the Apostles in Jerusalem: "they gave to me and Barnabas the right hands of fellowship." (Galatians 2:9). The Apostles appear to have practised a form of laying on of hands identified with the Temple priesthood:

"He is to lay both hands on the head of the live goat and confess over it all the wickedness and rebellion of the Israelites—all their sins—and put them on the goat's head. He shall send the goat away into the wilderness in the care of someone appointed for the task." Leviticus 16:21

Thus, while the rehabilitation of Israel began with the purification that came with the sacrifice of the first goat ("the Sacrifice of Justice"), it was through the laying hands on the head of the *second* animal and its subsequent death in the wilderness that the operation was *perfected*. The imposition of hands represented the principle of bodily life and signified a junction of spirit with the physical body of the victim. The scapegoat was an interface of the physical realm with the ethereal demon Azaezal, a disembodied intelligence deprived of all help and consolation. It is likely that Christ encountered this "tempter" in the wilderness during his forty days and nights, since everything that Azaezal offered was sensory:

The Scapegoat or "goat for Azaezal"

"Then was Jesus led up of the Spirit into the wilderness to be tempted of the devil. And when he had fasted forty days and forty nights, he was afterward an hungred. And when the tempter came to him, he said, If thou be the Son of God, command that these stones be made bread. But he answered and said, It is written, Man shall not live by bread alone, but by every word that proceedeth out of the mouth of God. Then the devil taketh him up into the holy city, and setteth him on a pinnacle of the temple, and saith unto him, If thou be the Son of God, cast thyself down: for it is written, He shall give his angels charge concerning thee: and in their hands they shall bear thee up, lest at any time thou dash thy foot against a stone. Jesus said unto him, It is written again, Thou shalt not tempt the Lord thy God. Again, the devil taketh him up into an exceeding high mountain, and sheweth him all the kingdoms of the world, and the glory of them; and saith unto him, All these things will I give thee, if thou wilt fall down and worship me. Then saith Jesus unto him, Get thee hence, Satan: for it is written, Thou shalt worship the Lord thy God, and him only shalt thou serve. Then the devil leaveth him, and, behold, angels came and ministered unto him." Matthew 4:1-11

When the Hebrews rebelled against Moses in the wilderness it was over food and water. In response God sent fiery-serpents (seraphim, sometimes equated with avenging angels) to punish them with poisonous bites. The remedy came in the form of Moses' brazen serpent, the Nehushtan, which cured the afflicted who looked upon it. (Osborne, The Brazen Serpent: Order and Chaos, 2022)[63] In Deuteronomy, Joshua is said to have received the gift of the Spirit of Wisdom from God when Moses laid hands his upon him:

> "And Joshua the son of Nun was full of the spirit of wisdom; for Moses had laid his hands upon him: and the children of Israel hearkened unto him and did as the Lord commanded Moses." Deuteronomy 34:9

---

[63] See my *The Brazen Serpent: Order and Chaos*, Rose Circle Publications, 2022

The Brazen Serpent

It is interesting that Jesus was *led* into the wilderness. This is a clear parallel with the scapegoat. The blood sacrifice was to come later, but there can be little doubt that Jesus was identified with the victim upon whom the High Priest cast the sin of the people. When did the laying of hands on Jesus occur? That is simple: it was at his baptism:

> "Then cometh Jesus from Galilee to Jordan unto John, to be baptized of him. But John forbad him, saying, 'I have need to be baptized of thee, and comest thou to me?' And Jesus answering said unto him, 'Suffer it to be so now: for thus it becometh us to fulfil all righteousness.' Then he suffered him. And Jesus, when he was baptized, went up straightway out of the water: and, lo, the heavens were opened unto him, and he saw the Spirit of God descending like a dove, and lighting upon him." Matthew 3:13-16

It is quite possible that John's baptism of repentance was a casting of the sins of Israel upon Jesus ("suffer it be so now"). The descent of the Spirit is usually equated with the Spirit (*"ruach"*) of God hovering as a dove (Genesis 1:2). However, it may be a reference to the Temple doves sacrificed by his parents, since in Isaiah the dove is equated with suffering:

> "I did mourn as a dove: mine eyes fail with looking upward: O Lord, I am oppressed; undertake for me." Isaiah 38:14

> "And when the days of her purification according to the law of Moses were accomplished, they brought him to Jerusalem, to present him to the Lord (as it is written in the law of the Lord, Every male that openeth the womb shall be called holy to the Lord); and to offer a sacrifice according to that which is said in the law of the Lord, A pair of turtledoves, or two young pigeons." Matthew 2:22-24

If John the Baptist was not conducting a purificatory washing but transposing the sins of Israel upon Jesus, we can see how the Apostles may have identified the laying on of hands with a sacrificial purpose. The difference, of course, lay in Jesus' resurrection, which reversed the annual guilt offering of the scapegoat with eternal absolution.

Simony

It is likely Simon Magus did not fully understand Jesus' sacrifice, nor the power of transference of God's Spirit that the Apostles were imparting. Simon sought out the Apostles because he believed their powers could only work if transmitted with absolute precision. In the Acts of Peter there is reference to this incident which supports the Lucan account:

> "Say now, Simon, didst thou not at Jerusalem fall at my feet and Paul's, when thou saw the healings that were wrought by our hands, and say: I pray you take of me a payment as much as ye will, that I may be able to lay hands on men and do such mighty works? And we when we heard it cursed thee, saying: Dost thou think to tempt us as if we desired to possess money? And now, fearest thou not at all? My name is Peter, because the Lord Christ vouchsafed to call me 'prepared for all things': for I trust in the living God by whom I shall put down thy sorceries. Now let him do in your presence the wonders which he did aforetime: and what I have now said of him, will ye not believe it?" Acts of Peter ch.23

Might it be that the charge of simony was a glossing over of Simon's true motives? This has resonance if we consider that Jesus equated himself with the Jerusalem Temple: "Destroy this temple, and in three days I will raise it up." (John 2:19). For the Samaritans, as with the Essenes at Qumran, the High Priest Aaron held a particularly high place maintaining the Tabernacle and lighting in the Holy of Holies: "Speak unto Aaron, and say unto him, When thou lightest the lamps, the seven lamps shall give light over against the candlestick." (Numbers 8:2). The Samaritans and Essenes alike regarded themselves as "the sons of Aaron" and as "the Sons of Light." If, as some suggest, John the Baptist was associated with the Essene community, then it is not beyond the realm of possibility that Simon of Gitta was too. If so, he would have regarded himself as being part of a select group entitled to minister to the Temple. (Encyclopedia Britannica)[64]

The Temple priests also conveyed the power of transference through ordination and blessings. A newly initiated priest received light and purification in the laying on of hands by the High Priest. (Osborne, The Lessons of Lyons, 2021). The intermediary nature of priesthood is the key point: it purports to bridge this world and the next through sacramental ritual, and which is something that unauthorised - non-ordained- persons are unable to do. It is therefore conceivable that Simon regarded the imposition of the Apostles' hands as a type of ordination. In his mind this may have been akin to the power the High Priest exercised at Yom Kippur to bind Azaezal.

> "[T]he exorcist has to achieve three things: he must repair his patient's aura, clear the atmosphere of his environment, and break his contact with the forces that are causing the trouble. These three things are interdependent."[65]

The above quote from Dion Fortune puts into context what is first required for an effective exorcism. We know that Philip the Evangelist was busy exorcising demons in Samaria, although the Book of Acts is silent regarding Simon doing so (we merely hear of him "bewitching" people and calling himself a "great one"). (Acts 8:9) It is certainly the case that in the Judaism of the time a state of purity was obtained through the Temple cult. Might the passage in 1 Enoch 13:1-2

---

[64] www.britannica/topic.torah
[65] Op. Cit. Fortune p.47

preserve part of the High Priest's prayer?[66] If so, perhaps Simon Magus identified himself as someone who, having neglected the essential practices of his faith, had to undergo atonement? For which, of course, the imposition of hands was necessary. Might this be the origin of the later heresiological statements that Simon claimed to be a messiah? Mere conjecture, but a state of moral disintegration and spiritual abandonment is hinted at in Acts, and which finds full expression in the later non-canonical traditions concerning him. Is this an end of it? Possibly not, because Simon more likely interpreted the laying on of hands as a transmission of magical powers.

It is generally accepted in initiatory magic that two wands or staves are required, as in modern Freemasonry. In first century Judaism, these were symbolised by the twin pillars of the Temple, Boaz and Jachin. However it also needs to be recalled that both Moses and Aaron each held a magical staff. These wands represented the fiery water of the Divine substance, represented by the combination of the pillar of fire and the pillar of cloud (water) leading the Hebrews from their captivity:

> "For the Lord thy God is a consuming fire, even a jealous God Deuteronomy." 4:24

> "Understand therefore this day, that the Lord thy God is he which goeth over before thee; as a consuming fire he shall destroy them, and he

---

[66] "Then Enoch, passing on, said to Azazel: Thou shalt not obtain peace. A great sentence is gone forth against thee. He shall bind thee; neither shall relief, mercy, and supplication be thine, on account of the oppression which thou hast taught."

shall bring them down before thy face: so shalt thou drive them out, and destroy them quickly, as the Lord hath said unto thee." Deuteronomy 9:3

"O Lord, the hope of Israel, all that forsake thee shall be ashamed, and they that depart from me shall be written in the earth, because they have forsaken the Lord, the fountain of living waters." Jeremiah 17:13

The two wands are also figuratively present in the cross too, representing Christ's mastery over nature in his death and resurrection. It is not altogether out of the question that Simon interpreted the cross with the sacred tau, the final letter of the Hebrew alphabet, symbolic of the four corners of the earth, the four elements and the angelic powers ruling over them (the names of which are invoked in transcendental magic, then as now).

In ancient Jewish cosmogony, "the four sparks of godliness" were applied to the tau, an allusion to the classical elements of fire, wind, earth and water, believed to be the signature of God embedded in the universe. In Jewish tradition the letter also represents the word *emes* ("truth"). The cross of crucifixion was therefore often equated with the letter tau long before Christianity, but that it represented elemental nature there can be little doubt. In Jewish belief the shape of the cross was also regarded as a sign of the everlasting covenant and became a token or sigil of God's power over life and death. The following passage from the book of Ezekiel describes the prophet's vision of the destruction of Jerusalem by the "heavenly executioners", who were only to spare those who wore the mark of the tau:

> "Go all through Jerusalem and mark a "Tau" on the foreheads of all who deplore and disapprove of all the evil practices in the city."
> I heard him say to the others, "Follow him through the city and strike. Show neither pity nor mercy, kill and exterminate them all. But do not touch anyone with the sign of the Tau." Ezekiel 9:4

For a god-fearing Jew or Samaritan of the time, the laying on hands to impart the sigil or mark of the tau would have been highly significant. Also, if Simon was a practiser of magic, as Acts tells us, then he would have identified the laying on of hands as an initiatory act. There is, however, no particular reason for us to assume that he had any significant appreciation of the true meaning of the Gospel as a fulfilment of the Law and prophecy.

Purification

Writing in the late fifth century, Dionysius the Aeropagite hints at a tradition that casts further light on Simon's cosmogony:

> "I hold, therefore, that those who are being purified ought to be wholly perfected and free from all taint of unlikeness; those who are illuminated should be filled full with Divine Light, ascending to the contemplative state and power with the most pure eyes of the mind; those who are being initiated, holding themselves apart from all imperfection, should become participators in the Divine Wisdom which they have

contemplated. Further it is meet that those who purify should bestow upon others from their abundance of purity their own holiness: those who illuminate, as possessing more luminous intelligence, duly receiving and again shedding forth the light, and joyously filled with holy brightness, should impart their own overflowing light to those worthy of it; finally, those who make perfect, being skilled in the mystical participations, should lead to that consummation those who are perfected by the most holy initiation of the knowledge of holy things which they have contemplated."[67] Dionysius the Aeropagite.

For the Apostles, this imparting of "light" through the imposition of hands was an outpouring of the Holy Spirit, a supernatural event. If we consider carefully the words used in the New Testament for this phenomena, we can detect evidence of its practical application by transmission from one adept to another:

- "And having prayed (προσευξάμενοι, *proseuxamenoi*) they laid on them their hands (χεῖρας, *cheiras*)." Acts 6:6
- "They then began (ἐπετίθεσαν, *epetithesan*) laying hands on them and they received (ἐλάμβανον *elambanon*) the Holy Ghost." Acts 8:18
- "Give me also this power (ἐξουσίαν, *exousian*), that on whomsoever I lay (ἐπιθῶ epithō) hands, he may receive the Holy Ghost." Acts 8:19
- "Then having fasted (νηστεύσαντες, *nēsteusantes*) and prayed they placed (προσευξάμενοι,

---

[67] Dionysius the Aeropagite, *The Celestial Hierarchy*, ch.3, p.10

- *proseuxamenoi*) their hands on them, and they let them go." Acts 13:13
- "Do not be negligent (ἀμέλει, *amelei*) with the gift in you (ἐν σοὶ χαρίσματος), which was given (ἐδόθη, *edothē*) by the laying on of hands of the elderhood." 1 Timothy 4:14
- "Lay hands hastily (ταχέως, *tacheōs*) on no one, neither be partaker of other men's sins." 1 Timothy 5:22
- "I fell (ἔπεσα, *epesa*) at the feet of him as though dead, and he put his right hand on me." Revelation 1:17

Certain words in the above verses should begin to convey to the reader exactly what it was Simon Magus was seeking - and how. Aside from fasting, prayer and prostration (falling down), one commonality is the imposition of hands. It is unclear if this was a single hand or a pair of hands (i.e. by one individual), or a single hand by each member of a group of initiators (bearing in mind that in Revelation it is a single right hand laid upon John of Patmos by Christ). In Galatians Paul asserts it was the right hand of each.[68] The laying of lands in Acts 8:18 and 1 Timothy 5:22 suggests a communal laying on of hands by the elders of the community. There is, however, always a physical touching.

In three of the above passages, we read of the "receipt" of the Holy Spirit, and Paul refers to this in one passage as "a gift" (*charismatos*). He also adds that the laying on of hands should not be conducted hastily, neither should the bestowers partake in other men's sins. In other words, there is still a purificatory element to it. The expression "neither be partaker" (or "do not

---

[68] Galatians 2:9

share", *mede koinōnei*) indicates the risk or possibility of the transference of negative influences by the imparter. This mirrors what we know about the passing of sin from the High Priest to the scapegoat. Hence the requirement, perhaps, for a purificatory baptism prior to the laying on of hands, as suggested in Acts chapter 8. There are indications in the passage in the book of Revelation of prostration, perhaps even entering a state of unconsciousness akin to death, reminiscent of the cultic initiation ceremonies of the ancient mystery cults, wherein initiates were led to a state close to death. There are also examples of prayers or invocatory words being spoken before the laying on of hands.

Essentially, if we consider the aggregate themes of touching, authority and the imparting of an exteriorized spiritual force as if ectoplasm (a substance or spiritual energy), then we are looking at the transmission of supernatural powers. There does not appear to be anything conventionally theurgical about the likely ceremony: there is no evident conjuration of the Holy Spirit, no invocations and no appeal to angelic entities. The laying on of hands is therefore of quite a different type than practical magic. The latter may perhaps be found in the miracles, be they exorcisms, raising the dead, glossolalia (the speaking and interpretation of tongues) or healing. Simon was almost certainly seeking command of such powers through initiation, and which brings us on to another point: which is that Philip the Evangelist was not one of the Twelve yet wielded the power to perform miracles. He was therefore initiated, as we read in Acts, and Simon was clearly aware of this. He correctly identified the laying on of hands by the Apostles as the means by which the "outpouring of the Holy Spirit" could be transmitted from one initiate to another.

I think it fair to say that Simon perceived the Holy Spirit as an igniting force, similar to the angel of the Lord who appeared in the midst of the flame in Moses' burning bush:

> "And the angel of the Lord appeared unto him in a flame of fire out of the midst of a bush: and he looked, and, behold, the bush burned with fire, and the bush was not consumed." Exodus 3:2

This perception would have been reenforced by the Apostles' description of the descent of the Spirit at Pentecost, which is preserved in the book of Acts:

> "And suddenly there came a sound from heaven as of a rushing mighty wind, and it filled all the house where they were sitting. And there appeared unto them cloven tongues like as of fire, and it sat upon each of them. And they were all filled with the Holy Ghost, and began to speak with other tongues, as the Spirit gave them utterance." Acts 2:2-4

We also have a description of a sound or rushing noise in the Acts' description of the conversion of Paul:

> "And it came to pass, that, as I made my journey, and was come nigh unto Damascus about noon, suddenly there shone from heaven a great light round about me, and I fell unto the ground, and heard a voice saying unto me, Saul, Saul, why persecutest thou me?" Acts 22:6-7

The principal elements of Paul's encounter with the what he perceived to be the Mind or Intellect of the Risen Christ Jesus were:

- the sound of wind;
- an explosive flash of light;
- the voice of the Lord; and
- a higher consciousness and visionary ability gained from his three days in the "third heaven."

We can therefore discern there was a process. Whatever happened to Paul, he became a changed man, possessing powers and a new light or knowledge of miraculous powers beyond normal human capacity. As with Jacob, who saw a ladder or portal into the heavens with the seventy-two aeons of angels ascending and descending,[69] so too did Paul have an epiphany of supernatural immensity. There is no reason to assume that Simon Magus did not regard the laying on of hands and imparting of the gift of the Holy Spirit as an astral initiation. For the record, it was common practise in the ancient world to subscribe for initiation into a cult, and he may not have anticipated the Apostles' dramatic rebuke of him for offering payment. The major and lesser Mystery Cults of the time, such as the Eleusinian Mysteries of ancient Greece and the Roman Empire were subscriptive, not unlike modern Freemasonry today.

The Holy Spirit

In 1851 the manuscript of the lost *Philosophoumena of* St. Hippolytus (died c.AD 236) was rediscovered. It provided scholarship with *a summary of* the reputed lost work of Simon Magus known as the *Apophasis Megale* (Great Declaration). Most interesting for our present

---

[69] Genesis 28:10-19

purposes is the Great Declaration's concept of God as "a devouring fire."⁷⁰

Paul's Conversion

The Simonian sect held Simon up as their founder, and they appear to have equated that fire with the "First Principle" equated with the *prima materia*. The Simonians regarded the First Principle as a self-regenerative and uncontained force, immanent within everything. Ultimately this was a doctrine of spirit locked in elemental matter. Now, if we consider Simon's background, it is possible that he regarded magic as a legitimate and lawful application of this indwelling Spirit.

We have seen that the imparting of the Holy Spirit as described in the New Testament was both an auditory and a visual experience (the latter perceived as

---

⁷⁰ Also as referred to in Deuteronomy 4:24

a flame), and both are reminiscent if not directly comparable to the burning bush witnessed by Moses. What this tells us is that Simon would be expecting to see a perceptible manifestation of a spiritual substance, like a fluid or fiery water. An auditory experience would also have been expected. There is a sense of the imparting of something tangible, and tangible things usually carry a price in this world. The question is whether offering to pay for that tangible "substance" was sinful or unethical, given that it was held to have beneficial properties. This is a point which Luke-Acts acknowledges:

> "And when Simon saw that through laying on of the Apostles' hands the Holy Ghost was given, he offered them money, saying, 'Give me also this power, that on whomsoever I lay hands, he may receive the Holy Ghost.'" Acts 8:18-19

Are these the words of a narcissist seeking to profit from the Holy Spirit, or the words of a Son of Light? Simon asked to be given the power to lay hands on others, i.e. to share the gift. There is no mention of him seeking to sell it on. If you reflect on this, Simon is not asking anything for himself, but acknowledges that it will benefit his practise of magic. This is merely implied, but gathers force in Peter's robust response. Peter, of course, may have made good measure of Simon and figured him out.

We must also consider the reference to the word "power" (Greek ἐξουσίαν, *exousian*), which can also translate as "authority." Thus, Peter may have become outraged at the request to share the authority of the Twelve who were to sit in judgement over Israel at the imminent Second Coming. Those "with the Spirit" acquired judgement. For Paul, judgement was what he equated with the intellect or mind of Christ. There is no reason to question that other early Christian leaders believed similarly. To know the Spirit is to know God, which reminds us of Adam's original state before the Fall, who had enjoyed all the virtues and powers of the aeons. Paul acknowledged the intimacy of the Spirit in man with the unfathomable Mind of God. Therein lay the source of the power and authority of which he spoke. Paul almost certainly believed that being "at one" with the Mind of Christ was a gateway to recovering man's original Adamic state. It is plausible that Paul's empowering of the twelve followers[71] with glossolalia was a limited transference of the gnosis of which he was "not permitted by Heaven" to speak (Acts 19:6). He may also have been replicating the structure of the Jerusalem Church and, if so, would have put himself in direct competition with it.

There is something intriguingly familiar about Paul's theology and the purported views of the Gnostic Simonians, which we can still observe in the surviving glimmers of conflict not fully expelled from the New Testament. More interesting still, is the encounter of Paul at Ephesus with a group of men who may have been surviving remnants of John the Baptist's group. The passage has eerie parallels with the encounter of Philip and Simon in Samaria:

> "Paul having passed through the upper coasts came to Ephesus: and finding certain disciples, he said unto them, Have ye received the Holy Ghost since ye believed? And they said unto him, 'We have not so much as heard whether there be any Holy Ghost.' And he said unto them, 'Unto what then were ye baptized?' And they said, 'Unto John's baptism.' Then said Paul, 'John verily baptized with the baptism of

---

[71] Acts 19:1-7

repentance, saying unto the people, that they should believe on him which should come after him, that is, on Christ Jesus.' When they heard this, they were baptized in the name of the Lord Jesus." Acts 19:1-5

Could this be Luke-Acts covering up differences between the community of John the Baptist and the Church? Might this passage be a snapshot of what may also have taken place in Samaria, hence Peter's robust response at Simon's attempt to "purchase" the transmission of spiritual power? What is singularly interesting in this exchange are the words "amazement" (ἐξίστατο, *existato*) and "signs" (σημεῖα, *sēmeia*) when describing Philip's miracles, because they are exactly the same words used to express the amazement of the Samarians at Simon's sorceries (μαγείαις, *mageiais*, literally magic acts). Crucially, Philip's signs were performed with "great power" (δυνάμεις, *dunamis*). This passage in Acts is critical, and I recite it again:

> "And Simon believed, and when he was baptized he persisted with Philip, observing the powers and signs in astonishment."

The table below outlines the full structure of the sentence in the original Greek:

ὁ		
δε		
σιμων		Simon
και		and

αυτος		he
επιστευσεν	episteusen	believed
και		and
Βαπτισθεις		when baptised
ην		he
προσκαρτερων	proskarteron	persisted
τω		with
φιλιππω		Philip
θεωρῶν	theoron	observing
τε		the
δυνάμεις	dunamis	powers
και		and
σημεια	sēmeia	signs
ἐξίστατο	existato	in astonishment

The passage highlights a number of key words used in Acts and throughout the New Testament when describing Apostolic miracles. They also happen to be shared with the description of the magic (*mageais*) allegedly performed by Simon:

i. σημεῖα (*sērmeia*) signs
ii. δυνάμεις (*dunamis*) miracles or powers
iii. ἐξίστατο (*existato*) amazement or wonder

The word *existato* is the third person singular of the verb "amazement." In Strong's Greek Concordance *existato* also coneys the meaning to astound. The word equates to astonishment and to be beside oneself in awe. There is therefore a sense in which the rather banal word "wonder" is wholly insufficient to convey something which more accurately conveys Simon's sense of numinous terror, even fear, at Philip's demonstrations of power. Yet the people he ministers to are equally astonished at his sorcery. In fact, the word is closer to the Greek word τέρας (*teras* "terror") performed to inspire onlookers; an extraordinary event with its supernatural effect left on all witnessing it, i.e. a portent from heaven to earth. The sense of *existato* in Acts 8:13 indicates an action in past time, describing an *actual situation*. This has to be a cover up by Luke-Acts, but why?

Prophecy

Philip was elected by the Church and then initiated by the Twelve as an almsman, along with six other Greek speaking men. The only description we have of his character is that he was honest and presumably good at handling money. Another interesting fact is that Philip was chosen because he spoke Greek.[72] This lends

---

[72] Acts 6:1-6: "And in those days, when the number of the disciples was multiplied, there arose a murmuring of the Grecians against the Hebrews, because their widows were neglected in the daily ministration. Then the twelve called the multitude of the disciples unto them, and said, It is not reason that we should leave the word of God and serve tables. Wherefore, brethren, look ye out among you seven men of honest report, full of the Holy Ghost and wisdom, whom we may appoint over this

credence to the legend that Simon studied in Alexandria, and was well educated, since the two probably communicated with one another in Greek. Is it possible that Philip's ministry in Samaria was restricted to the Greek speaking community there? The region had been slowly Hellenized since Alexander's conquest in 332 BC, and we know that Justin Martyr originated from the province. Philip reappears in later life at Ptolemais in Cyrenaica in Acts 21, where he offered Paul his hospitality: "Paul's company departed and came unto Caesarea: and we entered into the house of Philip the Evangelist, which was one of the seven; and abode with him. And the same man had four daughters, virgins, which did prophesy." (Acts 21:8-9) We have no further information about Philip's daughters, but the fact that all four of them prophesied is singular. Divination is a form of practical magic.

Divination, however we look at it, represents a quest for knowledge. It is a form of control over nature, and in that sense represents any other type of magic. The Hebrew biblical word for divination of future events is *kesem,* and that of clairvoyance is *nahash.* The root meaning in Hebrew of *nahash* means "to raise up", and it can also mean intuitive knowledge and/or natural ability. In Acts 21 Paul is arraigned upon leaving Philip's house by a seer called Agabus, said to have arrived from Judea. Agabus prophecies the near future,

---

business. But we will give ourselves continually to prayer, and to the ministry of the word. And the saying pleased the whole multitude: and they chose Stephen, a man full of faith and of the Holy Ghost, and Philip, and Prochorus, and Nicanor, and Timon, and Parmenas, and Nicolas a proselyte of Antioch: whom they set before the Apostles: and when they had prayed, they laid their hands on them."

and appears to perform an act of operative magic by taking Paul's belt to bind his hands and feet:

> "Coming over to us, he [Agabus] took Paul's belt, tied his own hands and feet with it and said, 'The Holy Spirit says in this way the Jewish leaders in Jerusalem will bind the owner of this belt and will hand him over to the Gentiles.' "
> Acts 21:11

Whether this was an act of sympathetic or talismanic magic we do not know. It was probably a benevolent action on the part of Agabus, because he is mentioned earlier in Acts as one of the group of prophets who travelled from Jerusalem to Antioch,[73] to warn Peter to stay clear of Jerusalem.[74] Ancient divination was practised in various forms including hydromancy, crystal gazing, geomancy, pyromancy and the theurgical conjuration of spirits. Divination typically involved the use of spells enabling the caster to learn secrets, interpret dreams, predict the future, to find things or protect individuals from harmful curses.

The sixteenth century grimoire known as the *Grimorium Verum* claims a tradition going back to King Solomon. What it tells us about divinatory lucidity is helpful, in that it may be induced by means of working with the spirits in the element of water or contained in crystals. (Waite, The Book of Ceremonial Magic, p. 314). The diviner therefore obtains answers from an invoked spirit. We simply do not know enough about

---

[73] Acts 11:27-28: "And in these days came prophets from Jerusalem unto Antioch. And there stood up one of them named Agabus and signified by the Spirit that there should be great dearth throughout all the world: which came to pass in the days of Claudius Caesar."
[74] Acts 21

Philip's daughters to make any particular judgment call in this regard, but Agabus certainly calls on the Holy Spirit for his divination, both in Acts 11 and 21, and he uses Paul's belt in an attempt to bind the curse that would befall him. This may be an attempt at abjuration, that is, the creation of a physical or magical barrier intended to negate magical or physical harm. Our task is made all the harder by the largely oral nature of first century magic, noting the striking absence of written theurgical texts before the destruction of the Second Temple, and which only began to develop during the rabbinic and later periods. That said, the Emperor Tiberius ordered the destruction of magical papyri, and much of the surviving material was destroyed by the Church in the fourth century.

In 2 Corinthians Paul expressly describes the *sēmeia* demonstrated by an Apostle and we can be sure that it was similar to the signs performed by Philip, who, if his four daughters were anything to go by, probably had an inherent gift that may have been brought out by training:

> "The signs of an Apostle were wrought among you in all patience, in signs, and wonders, and mighty deeds" 2 Cor 12:12

It is clear that Apostolic power was exercised for the purpose of demonstration. We know from Philp's demonstrations in Acts 8:13 that there was a threefold confluence of signs, wonders, and powers. As we read in 1 Corinthians:

> "My message and my preaching were not with wise and persuasive words, but with a demonstration of the Spirit's power, so that your faith might not rest on human wisdom, but on God's power." 1 Cor. 2:4-5

The description in Acts of the descent of the Spirit on the Apostles provides a tantalizing glimpse of what empowered them.[75] It was this force that Peter and John passed on to the faithful through the laying on of hands in Samaria, which also inspired Simon to purportedly offer them money in exchange for it, and which shaped Simon Magus' perception of what the Apostles were about.[76]

Whether Simon bought into the messianism of the Apostles is another matter, but the charism they wielded was transmutative, and was sufficient force to cast out demons and to heal the sick. In Acts there is an explicit connection to healing (physical and mental) in its description of this energy:

- Peter & John heal the lame (Acts 3:1-11; 3:16)
- Peter's shadow falls on the sick, healing them (Acts 5:15-16)
- Philip casts out demons (Acts 8:7)
- Philip heals the lame (Acts 8:13)
- Peter and John lay hands on believers who "receive" the Holy Spirit (Acts 8:14-17)
- Peter heals the lame (Acts 9:32-35)
- Peter raises the dead (Acts 9:36-43)
- Paul and Barnabas "perform" signs and wonders (Acts 14:3)
- Paul and Barnabas heal the lame (Acts 14:8-10)

---

[75] Acts 2:1-4
[75] "Then laid they their hands on them, and they received the Holy Ghost. And when Simon saw that through laying on of the Apostles' hands the Holy Ghost was given, he offered them money." Acts 8:17-18

- People who touch Paul's apron are healed (Acts 19:11-12)
- Paul raises Eutychus from the dead (Acts 20:9-12)
- Paul heals the sick (Acts 28:7-8)
- Paul heals all the sick on the entire island of Malta (Acts 28:9-10)

These were essentially demonstrations for the express purpose of proving the Apostles' *authority*. As mentioned above, the word for "wonder" is more accurately translated as "shock" or "terror". Such demonstrations (ἀποδείξει, *apodeixei*) of the Spirit were truly shocking, and not least necromancy.[77] Ultimately these signs and wonders served the purpose of establishing the Church and spreading the word beyond where the Apostles could physically reach. It is likely that the Apostles believed that being at one with the mind of Christ enabled the use of some of man's original, Adamic powers, wand which included the gift of life.

This is something that Simon Magus would have recognised as a Samaritan. For instance, the acquisition of the power of tongues by the remaining eleven disciples in Acts 2:1-4, and the empowering of the twelve men in Ephesus by the laying on of hands by Paul to prophesy in tongues, was a transference of the gnosis of which he was not permitted by Heaven to speak:

---

[77] In the sense of bringing the dead back to life, but which has strong Biblical precedent. There are explicit examples of people being resurrected from the dead in the Old Testament: the prophet Elijah raises a boy from death (1 Kings 17:17-24); and Elisha raises the son of the woman of Shunem (2 Kings 4:32-37).

> "And when Paul had laid his hands upon them, the Holy Ghost came on them; and they spake with tongues and prophesied."
> Acts 19:6

This wisdom is perhaps too precious - or too terrifying – to be transferred to anyone other than those who "live by the Spirit." For the primitive Church this meant living in a state of perpetual grace. While there is a hint of predestination and limitation of choice, it is clear that grace and salvation are open for all regardless of their spiritual gifts, but that the laying on hands was an act of ordination reserved for a select few. This explains why Peter was so aggrieved at Simon Magus' offer to purchase the ability to confer the Holy Spirit, assuming, that is, he did such a thing at all, least of all for his own personal gain. Peter's objections therefore appear to be based on Simon's morals and his challenge to the Apostle's authority. One can only assume that he was indeed running his own gig in Samaria, as described by Acts and Justin Martyr.

The Nine Charisms

We know that divination was practised in the primitive Church, along with other supernatural gifts. Paul summarised the "nine charisms" in his epistle to the Corinthians:

> "But the manifestation of the Spirit is given to every man to profit withal. For to one is given by the Spirit the word of wisdom; to another the word of knowledge by the same Spirit;. To another faith by the same Spirit; to another the gifts of healing by the same Spirit; to another the working of miracles; to another prophecy; to another discerning of spirits; to another

different kinds of tongues; to another the interpretation of tongues." 1 Corinthians 12:7-10

The legitimacy of these supernatural gifts is and always has been a matter of authority for the Church. In the catechism of the Roman Catholic church the charisms are granted by the Holy Spirit to serve the Christian community, with the exception of glossolalia, which interestingly received the special attention of Paul, who wrote:

> "He that speaketh in an unknown tongue edifieth himself; but he that prophesieth edifieth the church." 1 Corinthians 14:4

This emphasises intention, and reminds us that divination and glossolalia were widely practised in the Primitive Church. In time these were divided into nine charisms of three classes of supernatural power. The three charisms of the mind are wisdom, knowledge and the discernment of spirits. The three charisms of action are healing, miracles; and faith ("that faith that moves mountains" Mark 11:22-23). The three charisms of the tongue are divination (prophecy), glossolalia; and the interpretation of tongues. The Church teaches that receipt of these gifts does not rely on any form of invocation for their conferment or in the exercise of them.[78] It is, however, an area of debate if the early Church taught that charism ended with the death of the original Twelve Apostles.[79] However, in Ephesians we read: "to each one of us grace was given according to

---

[78] Romans 12:3-8
[79] Cessationists believe that the gifts of the Spirit ceased after the generation of Apostles died.

the measure of Christ's gift",[80] in other words, supernatural powers were transferred from Master to pupil. For instance, the charism of glossolalia could only be spoken under the direction of the Holy Spirit, albeit that in 1 Corinthians 13.1 Paul implies that tongues is essentially the practise of communicating direct with the angelic hierarchies (and in a quite shocking way for others to hear). This is why Peter did not attack Simon Magus for his sorcery, only for his moral conduct. To deny supernatural power would be counterproductive but, like the Pharisees to question its legitimacy was acceptable. Further, Peter did not seek to criticise magic because the people of Samaria and Rome could see it with their own eyes, understood and believed in it. Peter's message was that Simon's theurgy was being exercised by someone who was not living and "breathing" the scriptures. Why so? Because legitimate charisms and supernatural gifts are gifts of sanctification, as taught in the scriptures:

> "And the spirit of the Lord shall rest upon him, the spirit of wisdom and understanding, the spirit of counsel and might, the spirit of knowledge and of the fear of the Lord." (Isaiah 11:2

Quod erat demonstrandum. The narrative in Acts 8 now begins to make much more sense, and the demonstrations of miracles or magic by Philip, Peter and John in Samaria were the means by which each steadied the nerves of their converts. For the Apostles, who awaited the imminent Second Coming, strength was drawn from their inherent ability to outperform Simon with signs, powers and mighty deeds as the future judges of Israel. Conversely, from AD 70 the rabbinate developed in the wake of the Temple's

---

[80] Ephesians 4:7

destruction, and the parting of ways between Christianity and Judaism escalated. In Judaism, partly because of the loss of the Temple, and partly in response to persecution, there developed a written record of magic among the rabbis, who were keen to differentiate between legitimate, lawful methods and those which were unclean and therefore unlawful. On the other hand, as mentioned, many of the Greek magical texts were destroyed, and which explains why most of the grimoires today have a strong Jewish antecedence.

Sacramentalism and Magic

Regarding the sacraments of the Catholic Church, there are seven traditional rites, each of which is distinctly theurgical in nature and through which God is said to communicate his presence. These are:

- baptism: whereby the Holy Spirit "fills" the baptised with grace. There is therefore a transference;
- the Eucharist: by the consecration of the bread and wine a change takes place in which the whole substance of bread is changed into the substance of the body of Christ and the whole substance of the wine into the substance of his blood (The Council of Trent). Therefore, transmutation takes place;
- confirmation or the sealing of the candidate with the Holy Spirit. This is both an invocation and an act of sympathetic magic;
- in the sacrament of confession, the priest pronounces absolution of sins in the name of God by his power of authority. This is supplicatory;

- extreme unction by the anointing of the head and hands with the sanctified oil of chrism. This is talismanic;
- marriage as an instrument of sanctification. The rite is self-initiatory and invocatory; and
- ordination, where the priest becomes a mediator of the Holy Spirit. Ordination consists of two elements: (1) the laying on of hands and (2) a prayer of consecration. "Receive thou the Holy Spirit." The rite is initiatory.

The rituals of the Church are ceremonial magic. We see in all seven sacraments acts of channelling God's grace through invocation, evocation and supplication.

Peter's Baptism of the Neophytes, by Masaccio

4. The Standing One

Simon was not the only sorcerer impeding the spread of the Church. The sources we have seen thus far relating to first century magic suggest an emphasis on charismatic exorcisms and sympathetic operations. Amulets for healing, protection and curses have been found on fragmentary papyri containing invocations of the Divine Name of God and his angels. In the Book of Acts the mage Elymas, with whom Paul came in contact in Cyprus, was blinded by him:

> "But Elymas the sorcerer (for so is his name by interpretation) withstood them, seeking to turn away the deputy from the faith. Then Saul, (who also is called Paul,) filled with the Holy Ghost, set his eyes on him. And said, O full of all subtilty and all mischief, thou child of the devil, thou enemy of all righteousness, wilt thou not cease to pervert the right ways of the Lord? And now, behold, the hand of the Lord is upon thee, and thou shalt be blind, not seeing the sun for a season. And immediately there fell on him a mist and a darkness; and he went about seeking some to lead him by the hand." Acts 13:6-11

Pagan magicians were also the targets of heresiologist writers such as Epiphanius and Hippolytus. Yet the Church was unable and unwilling to criticise the imperial and official pagan cults until the accession of the emperor Constantine in AD 312. So their attention was largely focussed instead on the Christian Gnostic sects. Epiphanius' description of the cultic worship of Simon and Helena "as if gods" by their followers, suggests they were regarded as deities. However, this was not an unusual concept in the Hellenic world, and so the Christian writers attacked the conduct of these sects instead. That of the Simonians was singled out by Eusebius of Caesarea (AD c.260–340), who would write of their disturbing activities:

> "We have understood that Simon was the author of all heresy ... But those matters which they keep more secret than these, in regard to which they say that one upon first hearing them would be astonished, and, to use one of the written phrases in vogue among them, would be confounded, are in truth full of amazing things, and of madness and folly, being of such a sort that it is impossible not only to commit them to writing, but also for modest men even to utter them with the lips on account of their excessive baseness and lewdness. For whatever could be conceived of, viler than the vilest thing—all that has been outdone by this most abominable sect, which is composed of those who make a sport of those miserable females that are literally overwhelmed with all kinds of vices." (Wace, 1890)[81]

Eusebius also wrote that Simon put in a lot of effort in an attempt to achieve his ambitions, being "desirous of glory, and boasting above all the human race." (Wace, 1890)[82] This disparaging description reflects the narrative in Acts but lifts it up several notches, and which in turn remind us of the accounts given in the apocryphal Acts of Peter. Compare the above description with that in Acts:

---

[81] Eusebius
[82] Ibid.

"Then Philip went down to the city of Samaria, and preached Christ unto them. And the people with one accord gave heed unto those things which Philip spake, hearing and seeing the miracles which he did. For unclean spirits, crying with loud voice, came out of many that were possessed with them: and many taken with palsies, and that were lame, were healed. And there was great joy in that city. But there was a certain man, called Simon, which beforetime in the same city used sorcery, and bewitched the people of Samaria, giving out that himself was some great one: to whom they all gave heed, from the least to the greatest, saying, This man is the Great Power of God. And to him they had regard, because that of long time he had bewitched them with sorceries." Acts 8:5-11

Either the legend of Simon Magus was embellished by the heresiologists, or else this is a different Simon. Yet... and yet... there is a third possibility, namely that Luke was not interested in Simon's more lurid conduct, or perhaps Simon's behaviour and mission changed over time. We need to remember that the encounter in Samaria were some years before the events in Cyprus described by Josephus, or those in Rome as recounted by Eusebius and others.

Ambition

We have established that it is likely there was an historical mage by the name of Simon who was originally from Gitta, and who was proselytising under the pseudonym of "the Great One". Whether this was the same man described by Josephus or in the apocryphal writings is impossible to verify. Assuming for a moment that he was, then Simon appears to have enjoyed acquiring some impressive epithets as his career evolved.

For the Jews of the first century, the Name of God was embedded into the very fabric of creation, and the notion that knowledge of his Name could convey the power of life and death was well-established. The High Priest would recite it in the Holy of Holies for the protection of Israel. Just as God communicated his Name to Moses through the angel present in the burning bush, so it was passed down from Aaron through the generations of Levite Priests. Yet those outside the priesthood desired this secret knowledge too. The formal development of Kabbalistic magic and gematria was taking place around this time, a process that was expedited significantly in the centuries of antisemitic persecution and diaspora. We cannot be certain, but there is no reason to doubt the "sorcery" of Simon Magus was any different from that of other magicians practising their arts at that time.

Justin Martyr relates a legend whereby Simon Magus arrived in Rome during the AD 50s and by his "sorcery" established his cult. Yet if Acts is to be believed, he already had a significant following in Samaria and possibly one that was on off-shoot of John the Baptist's movement. There were many individuals and groups competing for followers in pagan Rome, although a statue ascribed to "Simon the Holy God" by Justin Martyr has since been established to be that of a Sabine divinity. The story of the statue illustrates just how significant the legend of Simon had become by Justin's period, and the extent to which Christian apologists were set upon undermining the Gnostic cults.

In the Pseudo-Clementine literature,[83] we are told that Simon wished to be regarded as "the Standing One":

> " ... he wishes himself to be believed to be an exalted power, which is above God the Creator, and to be thought to be the Christ, and to be called the *Standing One*. And he uses this name as implying that he can never be dissolved, asserting that his flesh is so compacted by the power of his divinity, that it can endure to eternity. Hence, therefore, he is called the *Standing One*, as though he cannot fall by any corruption." Chapter VII, Simon Magus: His Story[84]

The Church took a dim view of the magi it encountered, and the following examples from the New Testament highlight the perspectives taken by its leadership:

- St. Paul equates witchcraft to an "act of the flesh";[85]
- the account of a slave girl being forced to make her masters "much profit" by her powers of divination;[86]
- Luke applauds the many converts who had previously practiced magic burning their magical books of immense monetary value;[87] and

---

[83] So named because of the claimed authorship of the text by St. Clement, bishop of Rome (died c.AD 00-110).
[84] See Ante-Nicene Fathers, Vol VIII: Pseudo-Clementine Literature.: Chapter VII (sacred-texts.com)
[85] Galatians 5:20
[86] Acts 16:16-18
[87] Acts 19:19

- St. John the Divine stating that "nearly the entire world will be deceived by sorcery."[88] The result for the sorcerers themselves is "a lake of fire" and a second death.[89]

It is interesting that the priceless magical books mentioned by Luke were being destroyed by fire, to irretrievably remove them, and also refers to their monetary worth:

> "Many of them also which used curious arts brought their books together and burned them before all men: and they counted the price of them and found it fifty thousand pieces of silver." Acts 19:19

Given Simon's status and popularity - as recounted to us in Acts and Justin Martyr - it comes as no surprise that he would have taken an interest in Philip's "miraculous deeds." In Acts 8:11 it is stated of Simon that: people held him in "high regard, because that of long time he had bewitched them with sorceries." This is an overtly hostile comment, but indicative of the thinking of the author of Acts that nothing good came from Simon. That alone is highly improbable. In Acts 8:10 it is said that all social spectrums of society in the city held Simon in "great heed" saying "this man is the great power of God." Simon is said to have referred to himself as "the Great One":

> "But there was a certain man, called Simon, which beforetime in the same city used sorcery, and bewitched the people of Samaria,

---

[88] Revelation 18:23
[89] Revelation 21:8; 22:15)

giving out that himself was some great one." Acts 8:9

It is unclear what "the great power of God" and "the Great One" may have meant to the Samarians, but it is reminiscent of the grandiose claim that the Simon appearing in the apocryphal Acts of Peter made of himself, when he claimed to be "the Standing One." The epithet Great One was clearly offensive to the early Christians. However, the Greek phrase λέγων εἶναι τινα ἑαυτὸν μέγαν ("giving out that he was some sort of great one") needs further consideration because, if it was historically used by Simon for himself (and not, for instance by others), then we need be reminded that μέγαν ("great one") is the accusative singular masculine of μέγας (*megos*) which in Greek means "strong" or "abundant" (and not just "great"). Peter, after all, was called "the Rock" by Christ.

The Strong or Important One may have been a title of respect conferred on notable persons and village elders. It is possible that Simon was descended from a town notable, and perhaps the term was applied to him by others? Perhaps if he was referencing himself as abundant in his powers, it did not equate to going around announcing he was the greatest, like a particular boxing champion. It also needs to be noted that Jesus described John the Baptist as "the Greatest" (μείζων) in Luke 7:28:

> "I tell you, among those born of women there is no one greater than John; yet the one who is least in the kingdom of God is greater than he."

Certain Gnostic sects, such as the Mandeans, held John the Baptist up as the "Messenger of the Light" sent from the Father God to assist humanity achieve gnosis. Given that the Gnostics did not look to salvation from sin but from ignorance of true knowledge, baptism was deemed to be a purificatory rite. It was not initiatory in that sense but raised spiritual awareness or consciousness. Simon's baptism by Philip does not imply anything more than a purificatory immersion, akin to the *mikvah* bath ritual. Indeed, if we assume the baptism of John was of a similar type to that practised at Qumran, then it was not initiatory, unlike that practised by the Church. Simon's baptism in Acts infers he was acting solely from selfish motives, to extend his influence. There are always two sides to a story, and the arrival of Peter and John certainly has all the hallmarks of consolidation. It is therefore probable that Philip met strong opposition there, notwithstanding that Simon "steadfastly continued" with him (προσκαρτερῶν, proskarterōn), impressed no doubt by the deacon's supernatural "signs" (σημεῖα, semeia): "He continued with Philip, and wondered, beholding the miracles and signs which were done." Acts 8:11

In Luke 7:28 Jesus states: "I tell you, among those born of women there is no one greater than John.." The "greatness" of John the Baptist highlights the importance of his ministry to the earliest Christians. Yet Samaria was merely a day's walk from the Jordan where John had based his mission. Is it possible that Simon and his followers were emulating John the Baptist with the title and designation of the Great One? If John was "greater" than Jesus (perhaps if only in the sense of being before him) then why would Simon not claim that honour for himself on John's death? Perhaps he may have had a place of importance in the community based around John? As is always the case with a mystery to solve, the clue is in the question. In this instance it is the pejorative usage of a title of greatness being used by the community surrounding Simon.

Philip the Evangelist

If, perchance, the designation "Great One "or "the Greatest" was a title employed by the community of disciples surrounding John the Baptist, then this may give us cause to reflect upon what was actually happening in Samaria at the time of Philip's arrival. It is not improbable that the Apostles had to differentiate Jesus from John the Baptist during their mission to Samaria. This would have been doubly difficult given the obvious closeness with which Jesus was associated with John. Indeed, many were confused, and it was said by some that Jesus was John the Baptist returned from the dead. This was a direct parallel with the return of the prophet Elijah, with whom the Baptist was frequently identified during his lifetime. Even Jesus' own disciples reported that he was being confused with the Baptist::

> "When Jesus came into the coasts of Caesarea Philippi, he asked his disciples, saying, Whom do men say that I the Son of man am? And they said, Some say that thou art John the Baptist: some, Elijah; and others, Jeremiah, or one of the prophets." Matthew 16:13-14

The impression given in Acts is that Simon converts to Christianity because he is floored by Philip's superior powers and desired them. There is no hint that he was persuaded by the messianic claims being made about the risen Christ.

> "Then Simon himself believed also: and when he was baptized." Acts 8:11

This fits well with the description given by Justin Martyr that most Samaritans were following Simon's teachings in the second century (itself a reference to the known growth of Mandaeanism among the Samaritans in the region). Firstly, it suggests Simon may have remained a Samaritan, at least superficially, and secondly it implies that he may have developed doctrines of his own. A fading memory of Simon's magical powers and legendary healings alone would be insufficient foundation for the growth of the sect.

Another aspect smoothed over in the Book of Acts is the reason why Peter and the Apostle John "went up" to Samaria in the first place. Why both? And why do so when Philip was already there? Was it the pressure of persecution in Jerusalem that made them move, or did Philip require their help because his success was not as impressive as Acts implies? There is so much we can only infer from the text. The implication is that the Simon and his followers may have been remnants of John the Baptist's sect, and that the Apostles came to differentiate the Church from the Simonians and to put Simon in his place.

The Standing One

The Standing One was not therefore a messianic figure cut from the same cloth as the Jewish Messiah and Samaritan Taheb. To understand why, we need to consider Gnostic cosmogony. The early Christian polemic accused the Simonians of denying God was good, because the latter taught that the Creator was a demiurge responsible for fashioning an imperfect universe. As we already know, the Demiurge was a fallen spiritual being. In the surviving remnants of Simon's *Great Declaration*, we learn that he taught that he was incarnated as "the Standing One." This is a messianic claim of sorts, since the Soter of the Gnostics made it possible to achieve gnosis and reintegration with the Father God, or Monad. This highest deity was the

Perfect Intelligence, and whom the Gnostics believed was falsely ascribed by the Jews and Christians to the Creator.

Simon's description as "the Standing One" in the apocryphal literature implies that he was regarded as an emanation of the Soter. In Greek mythology, the Σωτήρ (*Soter*) was the personified spirit of a saviour or deliverer sent from the Pleroma (the highest Heaven). The Soter was understood to be accompanied by a feminine counterpart, the Soteira (Σώτειρα). The Soter and Soteira were sometimes identified by the pagan Gnostics with Zeus and his wife, Hera. There is good reason to suppose that Simon's consort Helena was equated with the Soteira, as we shall see in the following chapter on sex magic. As such, Simon may have fallen into the category of false gods identified by the Church and have been treated accordingly. This does not imply, however, that the Gnostic Soter was equivalent to the concept of the Messiah, and thereby with Christ. That said, the Hellenised Church rapidly began to formulate a Christology that moved away from the strictly Jewish concept of the Messiah.

The intense dislike of Simonianism by the early heresiologist writers was targeted out of disdain for the sect's immoral conduct, specifically its teachings on sex energy. To better understand the magic that may have been practised by Simon, Helena and their followers, we need to consider what was going on in Samaria during the first and second centuries. While there are invocatory and exorcistic hymns contained in the Dead Sea Scrolls located at Qumran, a general paucity of sources relating to this period creates a problem when attempting a reconstruction of what Simon Magus' practices may have been. Philo, Josephus, the Book of Daniel, the apocryphal books of Tobit, Jubilees and Enoch all reveal the influence of Babylonian and Graeco-Egyptian magic in the

Judaism of the time. The "wandering mage" was not a Graeco-Roman phenomenon.

For example, whether Samaritan or Jew, Simon would have taken for granted the existence of an angelic hierarchy surrounding the throne of God. This was a common belief in the first century and was derived from the concept of God being the First Cause of everything that exists. This was expressed in gematrical derivations of the Divine Name, and the names and the derivative numbers (powers) ascribed to the hierarchy of the aeons. These names were understood to contain all the mysteries of wisdom and were manifested in the seventy-two names of God mentioned in three verses in the Book of Exodus.[90] It was this tradition which influenced the apocalyptic literature of the period, including the Revelation of St. John the Divine.

The principal divergence between the Gnostics and Judaism was not only the former's belief that Yahweh was the Demiurge, but also that sin was not the fault of man. For the Gnostics, the world was an evil abode and a place of encampment for suffering and misery, not the work of a good and just God. The physical body therefore constituted the chief source of mankind's suffering and kept humanity in a constant state of privation. The means of reconciliation was through invocation of the angelic entities that had not rebelled from the Monad, or Father God. As a result, humanity had to make itself favourable to these good spirit mediators, because the Monad as the Perfect Intelligence was too pure to be able to communicate directly with such impure beings as people.

---

[90] Exodus 14:19-21. The letters in these verses were arranged into seventy-two triads of letters, and if the middle set are reversed in order, the seventy-two sequences become the seventy-two names of God.

Mastery of these techniques was held by the Simonians to have the following effects: (1) the acquisition of knowledge of the primitive state of the immensity of space and time; (2) knowledge of the emanated spirits, both good and evil; (3) knowledge of the original state of man as a spark of the Divine Being; and (4) knowledge of the Monad. The hope, the attempt and the supposed result of magic was to obtain the assistance of entities operating under the seventy-two names of God, to help the divinity existing in humanity to be realised and developed through the acquisition of such knowledge. In this process mediators many be sent from Heaven, the Beings of Living Light. Indeed, divine beings might themselves have become trapped in physical matter and repeatedly incarnate in human form. From this cosmogony the Simonians developed numerous rituals and observances aimed at fully restoring man's original state as a purely spiritual being. Magic then, was a means by which humanity was provided with the methods and abilities to transmute from one form of existence to another.

The origins of the story of Cain and Abel reflect the myth of the creation of human posterity by the Demiurge. Adam's second son, Abel, had been given direct knowledge of the Father God through a "cult" of magical formulations given to him by Adam. He learned that the demonic spirits were bound by the visual or acoustic manifestations summoned by the magus. Such ceremonial had to be precise and exacting, since it was required to ensure the communication with good spirits and prevent contact with evil ones. This was not regarded as a reinstitution of the original, primitive cult of the priest-king of the universe - Adam. Nonetheless, if practiced methodically, these rites were held to be able to reactivate the Divine energies within each person. These energies were required for man's first work - his reintegration with the Monad.

Such then was the theology and mystery of the "Great Power of God" known as Simon Magus, who believed himself to be an incarnation of aeonic Zeus, the Standing One, and whose mission was to find his way home to the Father God, accompanied by his feminine counterpart, Helena. This does not fit terribly well with the pernicious magician we encounter in the apocryphal works, but it needs to be born in mind that the ethical code of the Jewish Law and the creation myth of Judaism was abandoned by the Simonians, whose ethic of life would not resurface again for another two millennia. In this they differed markedly from both the Jews and the Christians, whose religions were not based exclusively on sacralised magic and mysticism but in a world intended to be a good place, created by a good and loving God, but which had become a place of suffering caused by Adam's sin.

Saint Peter Martyr Exorcizing a Woman Possessed by a Devil

5. Magic

There are many contradictions concerning the use of magic in the Old Testament. The attitude of the earliest Christians reflected the prevalent Jewish views of the time. As we have already seen, most forms of magic appear to have been tolerated by Judaism, provided they were not regarded as idolatrous. Jewish magic was required to have the right intention and theological bases to be considered legitimate. If Simon Magus existed, and if he was indeed a Samaritan mage, then he may have started his career well within the accepted cultural milieu in which he lived. The Acts of Peter preserve a tradition, also recorded by Justin Martyr, that "many" believed Simon because of his miracles (Acts of Peter 13). The text tells us that he practised necromancy, animated statues, concealed his appearance in a cloak of invisibility and could assume different physical forms.

However, necromancy and other ritually unclean or defiling practises were considered contrary to the Jewish Law and were particularly taboo. So too was mediumship:

> "And the soul that turneth after such as have familiar spirits, and after wizards, to go a whoring after them, I will even set my face against that soul, and will cut him off from among his people." Leviticus 20:6

> "A man also or woman that hath a familiar spirit, or that is a wizard, shall surely be put to death: they shall stone them with stones: their blood shall be upon them." Leviticus 20:27

"There shall not be found among you any one that maketh his son or his daughter to pass through the fire, or that useth divination, or an observer of times, or an enchanter, or a witch. Or a charmer, or a consulter with familiar spirits, or a wizard, or a necromancer." Deuteronomy 18:10-11

"And when they shall say unto you, Seek unto them that have familiar spirits, and unto wizards that peep, and that mutter: should not a people seek unto their God? for the living to the dead? To the law and to the testimony: if they speak not according to this word, it is because there is no light in them." Isaiah 8:19-20

Jannes and Jambres

The myth of the burning bush encountered by Moses atop Mount Horeb, where the tree was not consumed by fire, is an account of the interface of nature with spirit. It was therefore no ordinary, physical fire. The fire was the Living Substance of God, the *prima materia* from which everything in creation was made. Hence Moses' staff was able to transform into a serpent to demonstrate the power of the Creator God over all physical forms. The myth emphasises the point that both Moses and Aaron were adepts trained in Egypt, and vestiges of this tradition are preserved in Jewish magic to this day. No legend is more compelling than that of Jannes and Jambres, the names given to the two Egyptian magicians who confronted Moses and Aaron as a mirror of the eternal Hermetic principle "as above, so below." While not named in the Old Testament, Jannes and Jambres are identified with the magi in the service of Pharoah in the book of Exodus. They are expressly referred to in the early post-Second Temple rabbinic literature, and their names appear in the late first century New Testament epistle of 2 Timothy as well:

> "Now as Jannes and Jambres withstood Moses, so do these also resist the truth; men of corrupt minds, reprobate concerning the faith." 2 Timothy 3:8

In some rabbinic traditions Jannes and Jambres initiated Moses and Aaron before the exodus and, if so, then they would have received the transmission of their "secret arts" (Exodus 7:10). The interesting point is that the Egyptian magi performed exactly the same magic as Moses and Aaron:

- transforming their staves into serpents (Exodus 7:10);
- turning the Nile into blood (Exodus 7:22); and
- a plague of frogs (Exodus 8:7)

There comes a point where Moses' and Aaron's powers are clearly greater than that of the Egyptian sorcerers. In the tenth and most dreadful plague, the book of Exodus recounts how the Hebrews survived by the use of blood ritual and talismanic magic to protect themselves from the most feared seraph of them all - the Angel of Death:

> "Speak ye unto all the congregation of Israel, saying, In the tenth day of this month they shall take to them every man a lamb, according to the house of their fathers, a lamb for an house ... And ye shall keep it up until the fourteenth day of the same month: and the whole assembly of the congregation of Israel shall kill it in the evening .... And they shall take of the blood and

strike it on the two side posts and on the upper door post of the houses, wherein they shall eat it.... And ye shall let nothing of it remain until the morning; and that which remaineth of it until the morning ye shall burn with fire .... For I will pass through the land of Egypt this night and will smite all the firstborn in the land of Egypt, both man and beast; and against all the gods of Egypt I will execute judgement: I am the Lord ... And the blood shall be to you for a token upon the houses where ye are: and when I see the blood, I will pass over you, and the plague shall not be upon you to destroy you, when I smite the land of Egypt." Exodus 12:1-28

The first nine of these plagues are formed into three distinct groups. In the first, the Egyptians experience the power of God; in the second, God is directing events; and in the third his superiority over the Egyptian gods is displayed. The tenth plague is that of death. The difference, therefore, is that while magic can demonstrate supernatural power by the manipulation of spirit in natural, elemental form, "miracles" convey God's *authority*. This includes, of course, the use of the talismanic magic noted above, when the sacred tau sign is painted in blood on the Hebrews doors to spare them from the Angel of Death.

The division of legitimate and illegitimate authority in the use of magic is reflected in St. Peter's confrontation with Simon Magus, and in the experience of the early Church in its struggle with Gnostic magic generally. Hence why in 2 Timothy the author is comparing adherents of a Gnostic sect with the magicians Jannes and Jambres. It is a struggle we see hinted at a few times in Luke-Acts, and far more in the later heresiologist literature. Of interest in 2 Timothy

3:13 are the application of the words γόητες (goētes ("imposters" or "corrupt minds"), and πλανῶντες (planōntes, "deceivers", or "disapproved ones") identified with Jannes and Jambres. The shadows of this perennial conflict of legitimacy appear to be cast over the events recounted in Acts 8.

Sex Magic

We have already seen how Simon's epithet of the Standing One may have related to his identification as the Soter of Greek mythology. The sect purportedly founded by him certainly appear, by all accounts, to have given sex magic a prominent place in their path to gnosis.[91] In a surviving fragment of the *Great Declaration* of Simon Magus we read:

> "The Universal Mind pervades all things, and is male; the other appears below, the Great

---

[91] Interestingly, magical spells and the use of sex magic for the control of peoples' feelings are contained in Jewish grimoires, such as the *Sword of Solomon*, an apocryphal book of magic dating from the Middle Ages, but which probably incorporates aspects of Graeco-Roman sex magic: "If at a full moon you wish to seize and to bind a man and a woman so that they will be with each other, and to annul spirits and blast-demons and satans, and to bind a boat, and to free a man from prison, and for everything, write on a red plate from TWBR TSBR until H' BŠMHT ... and to stop up a mouth, and to converse with the dead, and to kill the living, and to bring down and raise up and adjure angels to abide by you, and to learn all the secrets of the world, write on a silver plate, and put in it a root of artemisia, from TWBR TSBR until H'BŠMHT."[91] The Sword of Moses

Thought, which is female, and which gives birth to all things. Thus, these, set opposite each other, unite and bring forth the Middle Space, an incomprehensible Aether having neither beginning nor end. In this Aether is the Father who sustains and nourishes all those things which have a beginning and an end. This is He who has stood, standeth, and shall stand, a male-female power, after the likeness of the pre-existing Boundless Power, which has neither beginning nor end, but exists in oneness ... Thus it comes to pass that that which is manifested from them, though One, is found to be Two, male-female, containing the female within itself. This One is Mind in Thought; for they are in reality One, but when separated from each other they appear as Two."

The antagonism shown toward the sect most likely derives from a misunderstanding of the role of Simon's partner Helena, also designated as the εννόια (*Ennoea*, "the First Thought").[92] Epiphanius describes the heresy surrounding the veneration of the prophetess Helena, although It is likely her legend originated in the description given by Josephus in his *Antiquities*, where the Roman procurator Felix employed a mage called Simon of Samaria to cast a love spell overriding the free-will of a woman called Drusilla:

"Now this Simon of Samaria, from whom all sorts of heresies derive their origin, formed his sect out of the following materials: having redeemed from slavery at Tyre, a city of Phoenicia, a certain woman named Helena, he was in the habit of carrying her about with him,

---

[92] Ibid.

declaring that this woman was the first conception of his mind, the mother of all, by whom, in the beginning, he conceived in his mind [the thought] of forming angels and archangels. For this *Ennoea* leaping forth from him, and comprehending the will of her Father, descended to the lower regions [of space], and generated angels and powers, by whom also he declared this word was formed. But after she had produced them, she was detained by them through motives of jealousy, because they were unwilling to be looked upon as the progeny of any other being. As to himself, they had no knowledge of him whatever; but his *Ennoea* was detained by those powers and angels who had been produced by her. She suffered all kinds of contumely from them, so that she could not return upwards to her father, but was even shut up in a human body, and for ages passed in succession from one female body to another, as from vessel to vessel."[93]

St. Irenaeus of Lyons also records the Simonians regarding Helena as an incarnation in human form of the "First Thought" and "Mother of All." Essentially, if we connect these claims with the myth of the Soter and Soteira - the provenance of the masculine and feminine forces within the godhead - the doctrines of the Simonians can be reconstructed as follows:

- the Divinity is comprised of a substance like fiery water, manifested from the Universal Principle or Perfect Intellectual aspect of the True Father God (the Monad);

---

[93] Epiphanius Ch.23 v.2

- the Universal Principle engendered the Invisible and Inapprehensible Silence from the Monad, known as the "Double-Divine";
- from the Double-Divine were manifested the trinity of Incorruptible Form, Universal Mind (the "Great Power") and Great Thought. These aspects of the godhead are equated with what Simon termed "He who Has Stood", "the Standing One" and "He Who Will Stand";
- in their perfect, spiritual form the "All-Mother" and the "Father of All" emanated the lesser aeons from the Divine substance of which they too were comprised;
- one of these aeons included the Demiurge, who made the world;
- Simon of Samaria identified himself as the incarnation of the Standing One, "the Father of All" (a common epithet for Zeus) and Helena with the Great Thought, a manifestation of He Who Will Stand and in its feminine aspect, the *Ennoea*; and
- there was therefore Divine sex energy manifest in creation from the outset. The desire of the disembodied aeons to incarnate was the catalyst for the Demiurge to rebel. The Standing One, Simon, and the *Ennoea*, Helena, were also now trapped in material matter and had to join forces to escape it.

There was therefore a philosophical and metaphysical interpretation given. For the Simonians, sex energy was contained in the principles of male and female generation found in all nature, mirroring the Double-Divine principle and the Divine Name of God combined. They associated seven powers with the Father God (six of which were his Mind, Word, Reason,

Reflection, Name, and Thought), and the seventh was his Image hewn from his Incorruptible Form. The Image was the Spirit, the fiery-water or power and substance of the Father God, which Simon sought to buy from Philip.

In this system there was an equal and well-balanced combination of masculine and feminine energy, reflecting the igniting life-force or sex-energy required for self-regeneration, and which found fulfilment in the incarnations of Helena and Simon. Thus, the Simonians believed that the creative, generative source of power "stood" or existed before the creation of the world. *The Great Declaration* suggests that their teachings relating to sex-energy - the harmonisation of which takes the initiate to the acquisition of perfect knowledge through achieving balance - was a two-stage movement from elemental form towards the formation of higher consciousness, which the union of Simon and Helena may have presented - the basis of their sex-magic.

Both the Standing One and the *Ennoea* were believed to have transmigrated from one human being to another and were required to rediscover one another. In her incarnate form, the Ennoea could never return to the Universal Principle until the lower emanations she engendered were reconciled with the Father God. Many of the seventy-two ranks of angelic entities created by the Great Power and the Great Thought to rule over the seventy-two sub-kingdoms of heaven created through the seventy-two names of God, were locked in material matter. with the various genii ranking beneath them. Simon most likely strove to invoke these in his magic. Such is my understanding of the Simonian system.

We now have a clearer understanding of why the early Church took such exception to Simon. It was a conflict over morality as much as it was about authority.

Whatever they were, the Simonians rituals drew the ire of the Christians. Epiphanius would write of Helena:

> "He had gotten hold of a female vagabond from Tyre named Helen, and he took her without letting his relationship with her be known. And while privately having an unnatural relationship with his paramour, the charlatan was teaching his disciples stories for their amusement and calling himself the supreme power of God, if you please! And he had the nerve to call the whore who was his partner the Holy Spirit and said that he had come down on her account ... For since the angels ruled the world ill because each one of them coveted the principal power for himself, he had come to amend matters, and had descended, transfigured and assimilated to powers and principalities and angels, so that he might appear among men to be a man, while yet he was not a man; and that thus he was thought to have suffered in Judaea, when he had not suffered. Moreover, the prophets uttered their predictions under the inspiration of those angels who formed the world; for which reason those who place their trust in him and Helena no longer regarded them, but, as being free, live as they please; for men are saved through his grace, and not on account of their own righteous actions. For such deeds are not righteous in the nature of things, but by mere accident, just as those angels who made the world, have thought fit to constitute them, seeking, by means of such precepts, to bring men into bondage. On this account, he pledged himself that the world should be dissolved, and that those who are his

should be freed from the rule of them who made the world."[94]

There is a similarity with the description given in the exhortatory poem found at Qumran, known as the *Thunder, Perfect Mind* scroll. This strengthens the argument that Simon may have originated in Palestine and enjoyed connections with the Qumran community. The text recites a female divinity identified with Wisdom:

> "I am the one who is disgraced and the Great One.
> Give heed to my poverty and my wealth.
> Do not be arrogant to me when I am cast out upon the earth,
> and you will find me in those that are to come.
> And do not look upon me on the dung-heap
> nor go and leave me cast out,
> and you will find me in the kingdoms.
> And do not look upon me when I am cast out among those who
> are disgraced and in the least places,
> nor laugh at me.
> And do not cast me out among those who are slain in violence." (MacRae, 2009)

Of Helena, Miguel Conner in his on-line paper *The Great Declaration of Simon Magus* states:

> "She had been abducted and ravished by the evil angels who made the world, and then she had passed into forgetfulness, to be reincarnated ever and again into one earthly, fleshly life after another till Simon, having

---

[94] Op. Cit. Irenaeus Ch.23.v3

himself entered the time-stream, came to earth to deliver her. In her, the Mother of all souls, he had redeemed all the souls of the elect, contained in her. And one might attain salvation, return to the Godhead, by accepting the saving grace of Simon Magus. Simon taught that his previous appearances on earth included one in Judea, where he had been crucified but only appeared to suffer."[95]

Epiphanius accused the Simonians of having

"enjoined mysteries of obscenity and—to set it forth more seriously—of the sheddings of bodies."[96] He also described them using the "snake-like filth of the aborted issue ... hatched from the infertile eggs of asps and other vipers." (Williams, 2009)[97]

The separation of the Universal Mind and the Great Thought was therefore analogous to the division of the male and female branches of humanity. A colourful and strong diatribe, but one which is suggestive of sacralised sex. Sex magic incorporated the occult use of semen for emanation and menstrual blood for evocation. Hippolytus described a rite of apparent sexual promiscuity by the Simonians. It has been suggested that the *Great Declaration* contains surviving

---

[95] See T*he Great Declaration of Simon Magus* - Aeon Byte Gnostic Radio thegodabovegod.com
[96] "*Emissionum virorum, feminarum menstruorum*"
[97] Frank Williams Trans., *The Panarion of Epiphanius of Salamis* Book 1, Boston, 2009, p.59 et seq.

remnants from a Gnostic mass, [98] and which Aleister Crowley attempted to reconstruct.

Irenaeus records that Simon was succeeded by an individual named Menander, who was also a Samaritan. This is interesting, because if true it has a hint of historicity about it. Why else would Menander be a Samaritan? We are advised that Menander was "a perfect adept in the practice of magic."[99] Irenaeus describes how Menander taught that the "Primary Power" (that is, the power or authority of God) had been sent forth in him as Simon's successor, "from the presence of the invisible beings" for the deliverance of all men. This implies a transference of power. Here the historical story terminates.

The Qliphoth

The Kabbalistic *Eri Chaim* (Tree of Life) allegorises the Creator's manifest energy. Its codification in the Rabbinate does not detract from knowledge of the existence of the paths of the *Yah Sefer* (God's Branches) revealed to mystics since the dawn of human consciousness. That there is a hierarchical path symbolised by ten worlds (the "sephirot") descending from the Divine immensity through the angelic realms and down to human beings has, in truth, always been recognised in the Secret Tradition - and long before Jacob wrestled in the dark night of his soul with an angel of the Lord (Genesis 32:23-32). Each sephira of the Kaballah signifies a type of force overseen by the Archangels. For example, Hod, the sephirot of majesty, splendour and glory, is said to be jointly governed by the Archangels Michael and Raphael.

---

[98] https://ecclesiaGnosticauniversalis.org/history/ *On the Origins of the Gnostic Mass,* in *Ecclesia Gnostica Universalis*
[99] Ibid. Ch.23 v.5

In the Kabbalah there is a corresponding negative image of the Tree of Life called the Qliphoth (meaning "the Nine Hells"). Qliphoth is an Aramaic term meaning "shells." These shells are the equivalent of the sephira and regarded as a representation of ignorance and suffering. They were consequently termed the *Sitra Achra* in ancient Aramaic (which means the "Other Side"). In the Hermetic tradition there is an equal and opposite of everything. As such, the practise of Kaballah is often an encounter with opposing forces. By the time of Simon Magus there was already a well-established tradition that sought contact with the fallen Archangels overseeing the dark realms of the Qliphoth, a system of spiritual thought and practise inherited from the black magicians of ancient Sumeria, and through them the Egyptians and Assyrians. Black magic was prohibited by the Jewish Law on the grounds of being unclean, unscriptural and idolatrous.

This did not prevent certain schools of Jewish magic seeking to gain control over these evil forces, in order to charge and utilise the corresponding force of good. This is another interesting aspect in the role of the practical workings of Qlipothtic magic, because command of it draws evil back under the ordinance of good. This is because the traditional path of the Kabbalah mirrors the so-called "unpaths" of the Qliphoth. Mastery and completion of all the paths is believed to lead to reintegration with God, since it forms the basis of perfection to have overcome evil in all its forms. Overcoming fear and repugnance of evil was the motivation behind Aleister Crowley's system.

Thus, by way of example, the Qliphoth corresponding to Hod represents lack of self-knowledge, being misled, delusion and untruth. It is the realm governed by the Archdemon Samael. MacGregor Mathers in *The Kabbalah Unveiled* described the demons of the Qliphoth as "the grossest and most deficient of all forms."[100] He equated the Qliphoth with the world of physical matter "made up of the grosser elements" and the abode of the evil spirits called "the shells."[101] The ten degrees of demons are the ten realms or shells of the Qliphoth, "the Kings of Edom." In the Tarot, the Tower card is often identified as representing the catastrophe of the "Fall" of spirit into a material state. Papus (Gérard Encausse (1865-1916)) believed that it signified the fifth element of the spiritual world, "incarnated" or encamped in the created universe. He wrote that the card represented the fall of man and debasement of spirit into the realm of organic chaos and destruction. (Papus, 1892) The flip-side of course is that God becomes present in our realm of Malkuth, the tenth and lowest of the sephirot in the Kabbalistic Tree of Life.

Dione Fortune identified two kinds of evil, namely "Negative Evil" and "Positive Evil". For her, Negative Evil was the polarising opposite of good,[102] whereas Positive Evil represented the demonic beings themselves. These Fortune equated with the "uncompensated forces" emanating from the shells of the Qliphoth and the "Names of Power" used in black magic.[103] These forces produce unbalanced evil, a residue of which persists even if balance is restored. Fortune would write:

> "When we consider all that must have been poured into these ten sinks of iniquity since the days of Atlantean Magic, through the decadence

---

[100] S. L. MacGregor Mathers, *The Kabbalah Unveiled*, New York 1912, p30
[101] Op. Cit. MacGregor Mathers p.30
[102] Op. Cit. Fortune p.41
[103] Op. Cit. Fortune p.42

of Babylon and Rome, down to the Great War, we can guess what rises up from them when their seals are broken. Not only do influences emanate from them which tempt and corrupt souls, each according to its susceptibility, but time has served for the formulation of evil intelligences. These probably originated through the workings of Black Magic, which took the essential evil essence and organised it for purposes of its own. The beings thus formulated assumed an independent existence, developed, and multiplied their kind."[104]

It is possible that when St. Paul set off for Arabia for fourteen years following his epiphany, it was for a process of self-exorcism, since "Arabia" may be an allegory for the wilderness occupied by the demons. Likewise, with Philip the Evangelist's departure for Arabia following his exposure to demonic forces in Samaria. We can also see how Jesus sending out the Seventy-Two Disciples in the Gospel of Luke was a means by which his selected adepts were tasked with gaining command over the forces of evil. They were sent ahead of Jesus to prepare his way, i.e. to cleanse entire geographic areas from concentrations of evil. First, Jesus asks his disciples to pray. This is significant and reminds us of the supplications of the Apostles Peter and Paul when doing battle with Simon Magus in the Roman Forum, as recounted in the Acts of Peter. Then there is the proclamation, when Jesus instructs the Seventy-Two to offer peace (balance) upon entering a household, since balance only exists when there is harmony. Finally, the disciples were instructed to proclaim the Kingdom of God. One must ask whether

---

[104] Op. Cit. Fortune p.42

Philip was sent ahead to control demonic forces unleashed by Simon Magus before the Apostles arrived.

Practical Kabbalah therefore seeks mastery of evil as a path to holiness, to which even the realms of the Qliphoth lead. If we consider the forty days and nights that Jesus spent in the wilderness to confront Azazel, one question that arises is the numerical significance of the number forty. In the Hebrew gematria the letter מ (*mem*) represents the number forty, which, numerologically, equates to the number four (40 = 4 + 0 = 4). *Mem* is also the thirteenth letter of the Hebrew alphabet, and Jesus was the thirteenth member of his inner circle, the Messiah to preside over the Twelve sitting in judgement over Israel. In the Torah the number forty represents spiritual ascent. The narrative of Christ's time in the Judean Desert highlights the place of the number four in the Kabbalah, namely the chain of Four Worlds (*Atzilut* the world of emanation, *Briah* the world of creation, *Yetzirah* the world of formation, and *Assiah* the world of action or making). Four is therefore the number of completion for the man freed from the sin of Adam. It is, as it were, to master the negative powers of evil.

This is the cultural milieu in which Simon Magus operated in Samaria on his return from the Hermetic academies of Alexandria, from whence he may have derived a mastery of the Qliphoth. In Gnostic Kaballah, it was believed that the Holy Spirit was exiled to the negative realms of the Qliphoth due to the "shattering" of the Divine Substance at the fall of the rebellious Archons. It was this "splintering" that caused "sparks" of the Divinity to become separated from the Monad.

The War Scroll

Simon may have been familiar with the sect at Qumran, and interpreted the Gospel in light of his own understanding. There is an interesting tradition in the second century heresiologist literature that Simon was a follower of John the Baptist, and indeed may have been one of his chief disciples.[105] It is certainly true that John appears to have enjoyed an effective and popular ministry, drawing attention from all classes of Jewish society.[106] The reason for John's death was probably because he became a threat to king Herod. If so, perhaps Simon's epithet the "Great One" in Acts was a title of leadership.

It is known that followers of John the Baptist existed into the second century, and some of them still proclaimed him to be the true Messiah.[107] If there is a potential connection between Simon Magus and John the Baptist, might this reflect both his willingness to undergo Philip's baptism and his misunderstanding of it as a purificatory washing? Might Simon's desire to

---

[105] The Pseudo-*Clementine texts, which* mention that Simon was attached to John the Baptist and was "second in authority only to John." This may be the origin of the statement in Acts that the Samarians gave heed to Simon "from the least to the greatest, saying, 'This man is the great power of God.'" (Acts 8:9–10).

[106] John 1:19, 24; Matthew 3:7, Mark 6:16 - 19

[107] The sect left Palestine for modern day Iraq, and came to be known as the Mandaeans, a composite religion drawn from Zoroastrianism, Christianity, Sarmatianism and Judaism, who believed in a perpetual battle conflict between good and evil. For the Mandeans, all good came from the World of Light ("the Living Water"). Conversely, all bad derived from the World of Darkness ("the Dead Water").

acquire the power of the Holy Spirit imply a desire to exercise his charismatic gifts within the demoralised Johannine community? Indeed, while the Apostles are disdainful of granting indulgences, they are quite willing to impart authority on those whom they regarded as suitable for leadership. This suggests Simon was not a convert, and as such he could never have been regarded as a suitable contender for initiation. Yet why? He was esteemed in Samaria and already enjoyed a following when Philip arrived. Peter's reaction is revealing, and he leaves the door open to Simon for a change of heart – suggestive perhaps that the two men of even temperament simply could not agree on matters of personal conduct.

Amongst the scrolls discovered at Qumran are *The Angel Liturgy* and *The War Scroll*. Each contains sections invoking the names and assistance of angels and which appear to have been the primary focus of worship of the sect that wrote them.

> "His knowledge at the words of His mouth come into being all the lofty angels; at the utterance of His lips all the eternal spirits; by the intention of His knowledge all His creatures in their undertakings. Sing with joy, you who rejoice in His knowledge with rejoicing among the wondrous godlike beings. And chant His glory with the tongue of all who chant with knowledge; and chant His wonderful songs of joy with the mouth of all who chant of Him. For He is God of all who rejoice in knowledge forever and Judge in His power of all the spirits of understanding." The Angel Liturgy, vv. 35-37

The War Scroll contains the following passage:

> "And You, O God, created us for Yourself as an eternal people, and into the lot of light You cast us in accordance with Your truth. You appointed the Prince of Light from of old to assist us, for in His lot are all sons of righteousness and all spirits of truth are in his dominion. You yourself made Belial for the pit, an angel of malevolence, his dominion is in darkness and his counsel is to condemn and convict. All the spirits of his lot -- the angels of destruction-- walk in accord with the rule of darkness, for it is their only desire. But we, in the lot of Your truth, rejoice in Your mighty hand. We rejoice in Your salvation, and revel in Your help and Your peace. Who is like You in strength, O God of Israel, and yet Your mighty hand is with the oppressed. What angel or prince is like You for Your effectual support, for of old You appointed for Yourself a day of great battle ... to support truth and to destroy iniquity, to bring darkness low and to lend might to light, and to ... for an eternal stand, and to annihilate all the Sons of Darkness and bring joy to all the Sons of Light ..." The War Scroll, Col.13:10-16

Transvection and the Demon Marchosias

There are a number of apocryphal references to the invocation of angelic beings by Simon Magus in the Acts of Peter, each of which reflect a similar utterance of the spirits we see in the Qumran scrolls:

> "[Simon said] ... but that I may not long endure him as an enemy, I shall forthwith order my angels to come and avenge me upon him." Peter said: "I am not afraid of thy angels; but they

shall be much more afraid of me in the power and trust of my Lord Jesus Christ, whom thou falsely declarest thyself to be." Acts of Peter 18

We also obtain a glimpse of what Simon's demonic helpers may looked like:

"Let great dogs come forth and eat him up before Caesar." And suddenly there appeared great dogs and rushed at Peter. But Peter, stretching forth his hands to pray, showed to the dogs the loaf which he had blessed, which the dogs seeing, no longer appeared. Then Peter said to Nero: "Behold, I have shown thee that I knew what Simon was thinking of, not by words, but by deeds; for he, having promised that he would bring angels against me, has brought dogs, in order that he might show that he had not god-like but dog-like angels. " Acts of Peter 20

What might these "dog-like" and ungodly angels have been? In Philippians there is an exhortation to: "Beware of dogs, beware of evil workers."[108] In the book of Revelation we are told: "For without are dogs, and sorcerers, and whoremongers, and murderers, and idolaters, and whosoever loveth and maketh a lie."[109] Aside from an obvious connection between sorcerers and stray dogs as an insult of perfidy and uncleanliness under the Law, in demonology there is a description of the fallen angel Marchosias, the thirty-fifth of the seventy-two demons who were cast from Heaven. This entity commanded thirty legions of dog-like demons,

---

[108] Philippians 3:2
[109] Revelation 22:15

who were fiercely loyal to the Magus summoning them.[110] We read of them in the medieval grimoires:

> "XXXV. Marchosias, a mighty marquis, appears in the form of a wolf with the wings of a griffin, a serpent's tail and fire issuing from his mouth. At the command of the operator he assumes a human form. He is strong in battle, gives true answers to all questions and is extremely faithful to the exorcist. He belongs to the Order of Dominations." (Waite, The Book of Ceremonial Magic, p. 43)

The apocryphal literature - particularly the Acts of Peter - preserve a colourful description of ritual magic. One interesting example of this is Simon's request that the emperor Nero construct a wooden "gathering tower" for the invocation of aerial demons, and in which we discern a link with the transcendental magic in the grimoires of a much later age which cannot be coincidental:

> "Simon said: "Give orders to build for me a lofty tower of wood, and I, going up upon it, will call my angels, and order them to take me, in the sight of all, to my father in heaven; and these men, not being able to do this, will be put to shame." Acts of Peter 21

---

[110] In the *Ars Goetia*, the first book of the seventeenth century grimoire *The Lesser Key of Solomon*, the fallen archon Marchosias is depicted as looking like a dog with gryphon's wings and a serpent's tail who, at the request of the magus, can also take the form of a human being.

Express in this passage is Simon's use of theurgy. The tower of wood is a tool used as a conductor to gather non-elemental forces unable to contact the physical ground. This is made unambiguous when Simon Magus says he will "call my angels." In order to project his will to fly, Simon requires to summon and cast his will upon entities that can help him levitate, and this could only be done through the invocation of the name of a flying spirit.

In a later medieval grimoire we can discern a hint of what Simon might have invoked:

> "Sabnack, a mighty marquis, appears in the form of an armed soldier, having a lion's head and riding on a pale-coloured horse. He builds towers. The reading of Wierus is preferable, i.e., Temples and Towers. But the reference is to the edifices of enemies. On his own part, he builds houses and high towers wonderfully."[111]"Vine, a great king and earl, appears in a monstrous form,59 but assumes human shape when commanded. He discerns things hidden, reveals witches and makes known the past, present and future. At the command of the exorcist he will build towers, demolish walls and make the waters stormy."[112]

Hence why the tower of wood was constructed, as it is likely that the entities being sought could not connect with the earth. We must again look to the later medieval grimoires for an indication of what the first century ritual may have contained. We find this art of summoning and compelling spirits in the fifteenth

---

[111] Ibid. P.223
[112] Ibid. P.225

century core material preserved in the grimoire *Lemegeton* (also known as the Lesser Key of Solomon):

> "If we would call any evil Spirit to the circle, it first behoveth us to consider and to know his nature, to which of the planets it agreeth, and what offices are distributed to him from the planet. This being known, let there be sought out a place fit and proper for his invocation, according to the nature of the planet and the quality of the offices of the same Spirit, as near as the same may be done. For example, if his power be over the sea, rivers or floods, then let a place be chosen on the shore, and so of the rest. In like manner, let there be chosen a convenient time, both for the quality of the air-which should be serene, clear, quiet and fitting for the Spirits to assume." (Waite, The Book of Ceremonial Magic, p. 92)

The Golem

There is an interesting passage in the Pseudo-Clementine description of Simon's ability to evoke demons, in this instance those imprisoned in elemental air. The comparatively early date of this literature makes it all the more curious, given that alchemical formulas for the artificial creation of golems with the "breath of life" given to dust appears in the much later series of rituals and magical formulas contained in the medieval Jewish grimoires:

> "And being thereby the more elated, he added also this: 'I shall now be propitious to you, for the affection which you bear towards me as God; for you loved me while you did not know me and were seeking me in ignorance. But I would not have you

doubt that this is truly to be God, when one is able to become small or great as he pleases; for I am able to appear to man in whatever manner I please. Now, then, I shall begin to unfold to you what is true. Once on a time, I, by my power, turning air into water, and water again into blood, and solidifying it into flesh, formed a new human creature—a boy—and produced a much nobler work than God the Creator. For He created a man from the earth, but I from air—a far more difficult matter; and again, I unmade him and restored him to air, but not until I had placed his picture and image in my bed-chamber, as a proof and memorial of my work.' Then we understood that he spake concerning that boy, whose soul, after he had been slain by violence, he made use of for those services which he required." Chapter XV[113]

This disturbing episode hints at blood magic, and also demonstrates a Gnostic cosmogony by Simon remarking that his creation was "a much nobler work than God the creator." The text highlights the creation of life from the fiery-waters that the Simonians taught comprised the Divine Being. Simon achieves this by transmuting air to water, and water to flesh. Traditionally, as noted above, golem were made from earth that was brought to life. The account in Pseudo-Clement underlines the existence of manipulative, elemental magic long before the existence of the grimoires composed in the Middle Ages.[114] The only

---

[113] *Ante-Nicene Fathers*, Vol VIII: Pseudo-Clementine Literature.: Chapter XV (sacred-texts.com)
[114] In legend, Judah Loew ben Bezalel (c.1512-c.1609) ("Rabbi Loew") was understood to have fashioned a golem to protect the Jews in Prague from

difference between a miracle and magic is, after all, that the former is attributed to supernatural forces sanctioned by God. In the episode of the boy created by Simon, God is taken out of the equation altogether.

In the medieval Jewish operations for the creation of such men of clay, a powerful rabbi would inscribe the Hebrew word *'emeth* ("truth") on the golem's forehead or may have placed a piece of parchment bearing the word *schem* ("name") in its mouth. The resulting creation could only be destroyed by writing the word *meth* ("death") on its forehead, or by removing the parchment from its mouth. The above account in Pseudo-Clement underlines the existence of manipulative, elemental magic long before the written grimoires of the Middle Ages. As Dion Fortune wrote:

> "The artificial elemental is constructed by forming a clear-cut image in the imagination of the creature it is intended to create, ensouling it with something of the corresponding aspect of one's own being, and then invoking into it the appropriate natural force. This method can be used for good as well as evil, and "guardian angels" are formed in this way. It is said that dying women, anxious concerning the welfare of their children, frequently form them unconsciously."[115]

The only difference between a go to miracle and magic is, after all, that the former is attributed to supernatural forces sanctioned by God. The biblical story of Exodus

---

a pogrom, albeit there is no historical evidence of this.

[115] Op. Cit. Fortune p.24

7:11-12 refers to the "sorcery" of the Egyptian adepts who confronted Moses and Aaron:

> "Then Pharaoh also called the wise men and the sorcerers: now the magicians of Egypt, they also did in like manner with their enchantments. For they cast down every man his rod, and they became serpents: but Aaron's rod swallowed up their rods." Exodus 7:11-12

Illusion

The ability to animate objects like statues is suggestive of illusion magic, wherein the mage uses spells to deceive the senses of others. Such workings cause people to see things that are not there, hear noises, voices or remember things that have never occurred. The cloak of invisibility is an example of illusion magic, an aspect of practical magic, like the ability to levitate, fly or transmute forms:[116]

> " ... those who adhered to Simon strongly affirmed Peter to be a magician, bearing false witness as many of them as were with Simon the magician; so that the matter came even to the ears of Nero the Caesar, and he gave order to bring Simon the magician before him. And he, coming in, stood before him, and began suddenly to assume different forms, so that on a sudden he became a child, and after a little an old man, and at other times a young man; for he changed himself both in face and stature into different forms, and was in a frenzy, having the devil as his servant." Acts of Peter 13

---

[116] Acts of Peter 13

One must take a view. For many, perhaps most, such claims are preposterous and reside wholly in the realm of fantastica. For others, magical operations are a very real interaction with the laws of nature; the exercise of superior natural powers and the result of a science where the will influences physical matter beyond its commonly perceived limits. Eliphas Levy (Alphonse Louis Constant) (1810-1875) was a former Catholic priest turned mage, and wrote that the only difference between a magical operation and a miracle was one of credulity:

> "Miracles exist only for the ignorant, but as there is scarcely any absolute science among men, the supernatural can still obtain, and does so indeed for the whole world." (Waite, The Ritual of Transcendental Magic by Eliphas Levi, 1896, p. 11)

I mentioned above that the magic of concealment or invisibility is a curious example of practical magic; a series of invocatory goetic processes. In *The Book of Ceremonial Magic* A. E. Waite provides an example of such workings from a fourteenth century grimoire, the *Key of Solomon*, which is likely to preserve vestiges adapted from a far more ancient ritual, probably in Hebrew. It provides a hint at the ceremonial ritual required for invisibility, which in Simon's day may have been preserved and handed down orally from one master to the next. The fact that a second century source is citing the practise if suggestive of something very much like it being used:

> "Presuming that the Key of Solomon is the most ancient of all the Rituals, it is there that the formal process first occurs. It is accomplished, however, without the intervention of a ring, by

means of a simple preliminary invocation, and an address to Almiras, Master and Chief of Invisibility, whatsoever may be necessary for the particular occasion, such as characters and circles, being left to the discretion of the operator. There is also a complementary process by means of a waxen image; it occurs in one manuscript copy and is given by the English editor. The person who has duly made and consecrated this image is supposed to become invisible when he carries it. If we now turn to the Book of True Black Magic, we shall find the first experiment adapted as follows:--Before making the experiment of invisibility these words must be committed to memory: SCABOLES, HABRION, ELÆ, ELIMIGIT, GABOLII, SEMITRION, MENTINOBOL, SABANITEUT, HEREMOBOL, CANE, METHÉ, BALUTI, CATEA, TIMEGUEL, BORA, by the empire which ye exert over us, fulfil this work, so that I may become invisible. The said words must be written with the blood before mentioned, and the following Conjuration recited: O Ye Spirits of Invisibility, I conjure and constrain you incontinently and forthwith to consecrate this experiment, so that, surely and without trickery, I may go invisible." (Waite, The Book of Ceremonial Magic, p. 306)

A flavour of how this illusory magic plays out can be gleaned in Aleister Crowley's 1905 visit to Mexico, where he was pursued by the local police and donned the cloak of invisibility to evade capture:

> "Recalling how he passed unnoticed on the streets of Mexico City, he thought to use that magic to get him out of this fix. Closing his eyes

and calling on his holy guardian angel for protection, he cast a spell of invisibility upon himself and slipped down the alley, past the crowds and out of sight." (Kaczynski, 2002, p. 152)

According to the Acts of Peter, as a demonstration of power Simon Magus levitated and flew at the Roman Forum. Let us focus for a moment on transcendental magic as it applied to flight in the narrative of Peter's confrontation with Simon Magus. In the Acts of Peter, the Apostle is challenged to a contest of powers, during which Simon levitates. As fantastical as it appears, levitation or flight in magic is not as rare in folklore as one may imagine. The practice is known as transvection, and it is not reserved for magic. Saint Francis of Assisi (1181-1226) and St. Alphonsus Liguori (1696-1787) are both said to have been able to levitate, indeed, walk, while in the midst of prayer (the latter being said to appear at different places at the same time); St. Joseph of Cupertino (1603-1663) was another; and as recently as the twentieth century Padre Pio (St. Pio of Pietrelcina) (1887-1968) was said to have levitated as if walking on air or water. There are others. In Luke 24:51 we read of Jesus' ascension:

> "And it came to pass, while he blessed them, he was parted from them, and carried up into heaven."

In Acts 1:9 (granted, it's the same as Luke) we are told:

> "And when he had spoken these things, while they beheld, he was taken up; and a cloud received him out of their sight."

This is about authority not credibility (or credulity). A common theme is the upward direction of the saints, whereas Simon's flights are transportive, he was, as it were, whizzing around the Roman forum generally showing off to make his point. Waite commented on this parting of "ascending" and "descending" magic when he wrote: "All occultism is part of the path of descent." (Waite, The Book of Ceremonial Magic , p. p.60). As painful as this is for those involved in practical magic to read, the hard, cold facts are that within the Judaeo-Christian tradition practical magic is regarded as the result of pride, the child of weakness, the original sin and that which led to man's Fall. There is, however, a contrary tradition within the confines of esoteric Christianity where magic is legitimized and employed towards expediting humanity's eventual reintegration with God. An example of which is the self-less Christianised version of theurgy developed by Martinez de Pasqually (c1708-1774). The scope of this book is too short to consider Pasqually's magic further, and the reader is referred to my introduction to the *The Lessons of Lyons* (Osborne, 2021).

The combined supplicatory prayers of Saints Peter and Paul cause Simon's transvectionary flight in the Forum to fail, making him to plummet to the ground. He would die later from the injuries he sustained:

> "A great multitude assembled at the Sacred Way to see him [Simon] flying. And Peter came unto the place, having seen a vision (or, to see the sight), that he might convict him in this also; for when Simon entered into Rome, he amazed the multitudes by flying: but Peter that convicted him was then not yet living at Rome: which city he thus deceived by illusion, so that some were carried away by him (amazed at him). So then this man standing on an high place beheld and

began to say: Peter, at this time when I am going up before all this people that behold me, I say unto thee: If thy God is able, whom the Jews put to death, and stoned you that were chosen of him, let him show that faith in him is faith in God, and let it appear at this time, if it be worthy of God. For I, ascending up, will show myself unto all this multitude, who I am. And behold when he was lifted up on high, and all beheld him raised up above all Rome and the temples thereof and the mountains, the faithful looked toward Peter. And Peter seeing the strangeness of the sight cried unto the Lord Jesus Christ: If thou suffer this man to accomplish that which he hath set about, now will all they that have believed on thee be offended, and the signs and wonders which thou hast given them through me will not be believed: hasten thy grace, O Lord, and let him fall from the height and be disabled; and let him not die but be brought to nought, and break his leg in three places. And he fell from the height and brake his leg in three places. … Simon in his affliction found some to carry him by night on a bed from Rome unto Aricia; and he abode there a space and was brought thence unto Terracina to one Castor that was banished from Rome upon an accusation of sorcery. And there he was sorely cut and so Simon the angel of Satan came to his end." The Acts of Peter, ch.32

The veracity of Simon's magic is not questioned in the Acts of Peter because, like the Pharisees before them, the Church Fathers claimed it was Satanic. What is most telling is not the negligible disparity between Simon's "magic" and Peter's "miracles" in type, but in its intent. While the Simon of the apocryphal literature cannot definitively be equated with Simon of Gitta (let alone the Simon of Samaria recalled by Josephus), we can nonetheless begin to appreciate the significance of this Simon as a "type" of mage encountered by the Church.

Nor was this encounter limited to the ancient period. The fifteenth century Augustinian friar Guillaume Edelin is said to have used ceremonial magic by invoking the name of Lucifer, through the use of a seal and characters written in blood. By operations - the details of which are no longer known - Edelin was purported to have been given the gift of flight on a magic staff. (Waite, The Book of Ceremonial Magic, p.155). According to Eliphas Levi, the great mystery of magic is said to be centred in the staff and rod of the mage. According to the *Book of True Black Magic* the staff should be made of cane, and the wand of hazel.[117] The fourteenth century Irish witch, Alice Kyteler (1263-c.1325) had a staff of hazel which she used to grease with a certain unction, and fly wherever she pleased. Examples from antiquity include the staves of Moses and Aaron, the two poles which supported the carrying of the Ark of the Covenant, the Nehushtan raised on two staves in the form of a tau cross.[118]

A well-known legend of magical flight is that of King Solomon's carpet, details of which are contained in the midrash *Al Yithallel*, itself inspired by Islamic fable. The myth of Solomon's ability to fly underlines the fact that he was deemed by tradition to have been a great mage, like Moses and Aaron. As with the grimoires, this reflected the belief that the biblical Solomon was given power over demons to help him complete the first Temple. Solomon therefore was gifted a flying carpet no less than sixty miles square in size. Legend has it that this carpet flew from Persia to Syria

---

[117] Ibid.
[118] Numbers 21:9

in half a day, reminiscent of Simon Magus' mythical flight from Tyre to Rome in a single day. The weakness of pride, however, seems to be the linking theme which separates the levitation of saints from the magi, as we discern in this Midrashic legend:

> "When God appointed Solomon king over every created thing, He gave him a large carpet sixty miles long and sixty miles wide, made of green silk interwoven with pure gold, and ornamented with figured decorations. Surrounded by his four princes, Asaph b. Berechiah, prince of men, Ramirat, prince of the demons, a lion, prince of beasts, and an eagle, prince of birds, when Solomon sat upon the carpet he was caught up by the wind and sailed through the air so quickly that he breakfasted at Damascus and supped in Media. One day Solomon was filled with pride at his own greatness and wisdom; and as a punishment therefore the wind shook the carpet, throwing down 40,000 men." (Jellinek, 1853)[119]

Casting Curses

The *Pulsa Denoura* is an ancient Aramaic ritual purporting to inflict death on its victims within a year. It invokes "heavenly executioners" to block forgiveness of the subject's sins, causing all of the curses named in the Bible to befall upon them. It is said to require ten men to perform the ritual. It is an example of Jewish magic and may well be allegorised in the myth of the tenth plague afflicting Egypt in Exodus. There would have been an imposition of hands on a blood victim to effect the curse, akin to a reversal of the Yom Kippur

---

[119] *Midrash VaYosha*

invocatory prayer. One must imagine that Moses and Aaron used the *pulsa denoura* to invoke the Angel of Death upon Egypt. The Aramaic word *pulsa* means "attack" and *denoura* means "fire". The *Pulsa Denoura* is therefore an *attack of fire* by invocation, and one which by tradition requires at least ten exponents to perform (reminiscent of the ten angels who brought plague on Egypt). The phrase appears in classical rabbinic literature, and the source for the ritual is to be found in the Jewish theurgical rites of the *Sefer HaRazim* and the *Sword of Moses*.

> "It should also be observed that experiments which have for their object an interference with the freewill of another person, such as that of seeking favour and love, are essentially evil experiments. I have now enumerated all the processes which are set forth in this "fountainhead and storehouse of Kabbalistical Magic"; it is for such trumpery purposes that the Magus is directed to undertake his laborious preparation, and for such also to put in motion the powers believed to be inherent in Divine Names, in long pages of pretentious prayers and in "stronger and more powerful" conjurations." (Waite, The Book of Ceremonial Magic)[120]

The *Sword of Moses* is an apocryphal book of Jewish magic, which might conceivably date from the first century AD. It begins with a description of the heavenly realms and angels, and provides various angelic invocations and theurgical procedures required to manipulate the fate of others:

---

[120] Ceremonial Magic p.78

"In the name of the mighty and holy God! Four angels are appointed to the "Sword" given by the Lord, the Master of mysteries, and they are appointed to the Law, and they see with penetration the mysteries from above and below; and these are their names — SKD HUZI, MRGIOIAL, VHDRZIOLO, TOTRISI. [CQD HUZI MRGIZIAL, UHDRZIULU, TUTRISI] And over these are five others, holy and mighty, who meditate on the mysteries of God in the world for seven hours every day, and they are appointed to thousands of thousands, and to myriads of thousands of Chariots, ready to do the will of their Creator." (Harari, 2012, pp. pp. 58-98)[121]

Magic, then as now, incorporated rites (operations) using sacred calendars and the invocation of angelic or demonic names. A requirement for magic in Judaism was for the command of these disembodied intelligences to derive from God alone, since any other magic was idolatrous and therefore prohibited by the Law.

Possession

The confrontation with Simon Magus took place in Rome, before the Emperor and a pagan crowd that was less precious about idolatry. It should therefore come as no surprise that, in the Acts of Peter, the Apostles are seen to demonstrate their powers in a radical, almost magical way. Thus, we see Peter restoring a broken statue of the Emperor ("And he sprinkled the water upon the stones, and the statue became whole" Acts of

---

[121] *The Sword of* Moses

Peter 11), and publicly confronting Simon by sending him messages via a talking dog, thereby mocking his earlier invocation of the dog-like demons:

> "And Peter seeing a great dog bound with a strong chain, went to him and loosed him, and when he was loosed the dog received a man's voice and said unto Peter: What dost thou bid me to do, thou servant of the unspeakable and living God? Peter said unto him: Go in and say unto Simon in the midst of his company: Peter saith unto thee, Come forth abroad, for thy sake am I come to Rome, thou wicked one and deceiver of simple souls. And immediately the dog ran and entered in, and rushed into the midst of them that were with Simon, and lifted up his forefeet and in a loud voice said: Thou Simon, Peter the servant of Christ who standeth at the door saith unto thee: Come forth abroad, for thy sake am I come to Rome, thou most wicked one and deceiver of simple souls. And when Simon heard it, and beheld the incredible sight, he lost the words wherewith he was deceiving them that stood by, and all of them were amazed." Acts of Peter 9

The event in question leads to the conversion of Simon's wealthy Roman benefactor, the senator Marcellus, to Christianity. We read how someone in the crowd laughed at this, "in whom was a very evil spirit." This individual transpired to be the servant living at the same house as Simon Magus and Marcellus, which suggests an infestation of malignant spirits at the property. The servant then recounts what the talking dog sent by Peter did:

> "And Peter said unto him: 'Whosoever thou art that didst laugh, show thyself openly unto all that are present.' And hearing this the young man ran into the court of the house and cried out with a loud voice and dashed himself against the wall and said: 'Peter, there is a great contention between Simon and the dog whom thou sentest; for Simon saith to the dog: "Say that I am not here." Unto whom the dog saith more than thou didst charge him; and when he hath accomplished the mystery which thou didst command him, he shall die at thy feet.'" Acts of Peter 11

The talking dog cursed Simon in the presence of Marcellus

> "Cursed therefore shalt thou be, thou enemy and corrupter of the way of the truth of Christ, who shall prove by fire that dieth not and in outer darkness, thine iniquities that thou hast committed." Acts of Peter 12

The dog itself is possessed by "an angel" acting in the Name of God. There are eerie resemblances here with the casting out of the demonic Legion into the large herd of pigs by Christ in the Synoptic Gospels,[122] and it appears to follow a similar trajectory, as the dog dies once its mission is completed. The operations are therefore similar and have the same purpose of tormenting demons and of cleansing a specific geographical location. Marcellus, we are told, later cleanses his whole house from any trace of Simon: ("For I took water and called upon the holy name of Jesus Christ, together with mine other servants which

---

[122] Mark 5:1-23; Matthew 8:28-34; and Luke 8:26-39.

belong unto him, and sprinkled all my house and all the dining chambers and all the porticoes, even unto the outer gate.")[123]

As for the dog:

> "[it] related what he had done unto Simon. And thus spake the dog unto the angel and Apostle of the true God: 'Peter, thou wilt have a great contest with the enemy of Christ and his servants, and many that have been deceived by him shalt thou turn unto the faith; wherefore thou shalt receive from God the reward of thy work.' And when the dog had said this he fell down at the Apostle Peter's feet and gave up the ghost." Acts of Peter 12

There is also an account of Peter enabling a baby to speak with "the voice of a man" to chastise Simon.[124] Marcellus' servant is exorcised by Peter, but then goes on to topple the said statue of Nero, a political act and capital crime, in which Peter is indirectly implicated! Peter restores the statue, heals the blind, and during this

---

[123] Ibid. ch.19

[124] Acts of Peter, ch.15: "Now the child whom she suckled was seven months old; and it received a man's voice and said unto Simon: O thou abhorred of God and men, and destruction of truth, and evil seed of all corruption, O fruit by nature unprofitable! but only for a short and little season shalt thou be seen, and thereafter eternal punishment is laid up for thee. Thou son of a shameless father, that never puttest forth thy roots for good but for poison, faithless generation void of all hope! thou wast not confounded when a dog reproved thee; I a child am compelled of God to speak, and not even now art thou ashamed."

scene of sublime chaos challenges Simon to a contest to demonstrate their powers in public. So, when Peter restores a dead fish hanging in a window back to life,[125] the outcome of the challenge was decided by the Emperor himself: raise the dead.

Regarding demonic possession, there is a common belief that evil spirits attach to people and, indeed, this is a very common view in most cultures in all times and places. The ancient world was no exception. Regardless of modern science explaining this phenomena as manifestation of mental illness, demonic possession is widely recorded throughout history and is just as prevalent today as it was two-thousand years distant. For this reason the Seventy-Two disciples Jesus initiated were "sent out two by two ahead of him."[126] Their

---

[125] "And Peter turned and saw a herring (sardine) hung in a window, and took it and said to the people: If ye now see this swimming in the water like a fish, will ye be able to believe in him whom I preach? And they said with one voice: Verily we will believe thee. Then he said -now there was a bath for swimming at hand: In thy name, O Jesu Christ, forasmuch as hitherto it is not believed in, in the sight of all these live and swim like a fish. And he cast the herring into the bath, and it lived and began to swim. And all the people saw the fish swimming, and it did not so at that hour only, lest it should be said that it was a delusion (phantasm), but he made it to swim for a long time, so that they brought much people from all quarters and showed them the herring that was made a living fish, so that certain of the people even cast bread to it; and they saw that it was whole" Acts of Peter 13[125] Matthew 11:23; 16:18; Luke 10:15; 16:23; Acts 2:27; 2:31; Romans 10:6-8; 1 Corinthians 15:55; 1 Peter 3:19-20; Ephesians 4:7-10; Philippians 29-10; Revelation 1:18; 6:8; 20:13; 20:14.
[126] Luke 10:1–24

number was no coincidence, as each of them equated to one of the seventy-two Names for God, the acoustic repetition of which invoked the Divinity to seal the locations they went. The seventy-two permutations of the four letters of the Tetragrammaton (YHWH) spoken in twelve different permutations, were the most potent of invocations for binding each of the corresponding seventy-two demons who had fallen from grace. This was because creation was believed to have been created through the seventy-two permutations arising from the various versions of the twelve Names.

Each disciple was a powerful exorcist sent out "into the wilderness" of the world to restrain them. The invocation of the Name of God confers significant spiritual power, and the pairing of the Seventy-Two men into thirty-six groups was for the express purpose of spiritually cleansing areas where demonic infestation was rife. No doubt Samaria was firmly on the list. Little wonder, then, that the polemic aimed at Simon Magus rarely denied the authenticity of his magical operations, although there were occasional cries of trickery.

Let us look at the full text of Luke 10:1-22 in full, where Jesus sends out the Seventy-Two, as it is revealing:

> "And after these things the Lord appointed also other seventy-two: and he sent them two and two before his face into every city and place whither he himself was to come. And he said to them: 'The harvest indeed is great, but the labourers are few. Pray ye therefore the Lord of the harvest, that he send labourers into his harvest. Go: Behold I send you as lambs among wolves. Carry neither purse, nor scrip, nor shoes; and salute no man by the way. Into whatsoever house you enter, first say: Peace be to this house. And if the son of peace be

there, your peace shall rest upon him; but if not, it shall return to you. And in the same house, remain, eating and drinking such things as they have: for the labourer is worthy of his hire. Remove not from house to house. And into what city soever you enter, and they receive you, eat such things as are set before you. And heal the sick that are therein and say to them: The kingdom of God is come nigh unto you. But into whatsoever city you enter, and they receive you not, going forth into the streets thereof, say: Even the very dust of your city that cleaveth to us, we wipe off against you. Yet know this, that the kingdom of God is at hand.

"I say to you, it shall be more tolerable at that day for Sodom, than for that city. Woe to thee, Corozain, woe to thee, Bethsaida. For if in Tyre and Sidon had been wrought the mighty works that have been wrought in you, they would have done penance long ago, sitting in sackcloth and ashes. But it shall be more tolerable for Tyre and Sidon at the judgement, than for you. And thou, Capharnaum, which art exalted unto heaven, thou shalt be thrust down to hell. He that heareth you, heareth me; and he that despiseth you, despiseth me; and he that despiseth me, despiseth him that sent me.'

"And the seventy-two returned with joy, saying: 'Lord, the devils also are subject to us in thy name.' And he said to them: 'I saw Satan like lightning falling from heaven. Behold, I have given you power to tread upon serpents and scorpions, and upon all the power of the enemy: and nothing shall hurt you. But yet rejoice not in this, that spirits are subject unto you; but rejoice in this, that your names are written in heaven.' In that same hour, he rejoiced in the Holy Ghost, and said: 'I confess to

thee, O Father, Lord of heaven and earth, because thou hast hidden these things from the wise and prudent, and hast revealed them to little ones. Yea, Father, for so it hath seemed good in thy sight.'"
Luke 10:1-22

A similar commissioning occurs in Matthew 10:5-42, with the Twelve Disciples sent out to heal and cast out demons The main difference is that Jesus instructed they were to preach only in Galilee - avoiding Samaria:

> "Go not into the way of the Gentiles, and into any city of the Samaritans enter ye not."

This could be – and usually is – put down to the tensions between the religious Samaritans and Jews. However, by now you will appreciate that the thrust of the accounts in both Luke and Matthew is what it tells us about the spiritual distress in Samaria, and the infestation of demonic entities afflicting the people there. The mission of the Twelve in Galilee was clearly to cleanse that region in readiness for Christ's ministry there. Thus, in the Lucan account we discern the following points:

- the pairing of exorcists (as we see in the combination of Peter and Paul in opposing Simon Magus in Rome);
- the specific command to carry no money (clearly unlike Simon Magus, of whom with some confidence it can be said carried a full purse);
- a mission of exorcism as a precursor of the imminent Day of Judgment;
- the Seventy-Two and the Twelve subject demonic forces by the invocation of the Divine Name;

- Jesus remarks that he sees Satan cast from Heaven like "a bolt of lightning." Here we see a direct parallel of Satan and the seventy-two archons cast from Heaven;
- the Seventy-Two and the Twelve are given the express *power* to tread on these "serpents" and "upon all the power of the enemy." The evil spirits are subject to them; and
- there is a prayer of thanksgiving to God.

The reality of magic is not in question in the New Testament. The defamatory polemic of the early Church was instead directed at the provenance of Simon's power and use of black magic. He is "the angel of Satan" (Acts of Peter ch.32), and the Simon in which "there are two essences, of man and of the devil" (Acts of Peter ch.17). One office not included in the seven official sacraments of the Catholic Church is that of exorcism. In 1999 a revised version of the Rite of Exorcism was issued which included the "Leonine Prayers"[127] of Pope Leo XIII, of which his invocation of Saint Michael is one of the most prominent. This was added in 1886 to the prayers to be spoken after each low mass.[128] Indeed, it is said that Pope Leo composed

---

[127] The Leonine Prayers consist of three Hail Marys, a Salve Regina and a prayer for the conversion of sinners and the liberty of the Catholic Church. The prayer to St. Michael was added later.

[128] "Blessed Michael, archangel, defend us in the hour of conflict. Be our safeguard against the wickedness and snares of the devil (may God restrain him, we humbly pray):and do thou, O Prince of the heavenly host, by the power of God thrust Satan down to hell and with him those other wicked spirits who wander through the world for the ruin of souls. Amen."

this prayer having seen a vision of Satan conversing with God over the city of Rome in the year 1884, during the troubled period following Italian unification. Curiously, Leo XIII is buried at the papal Archbasilica of St. John Lateran, where the skulls of Saints Peter and Paul are said to be interred.

In 1890 another prayer to the Archangel Michael was added to the rite of exorcism in the *Acta Sanctae Sedis*. In *Exorcismus in Satanam et angelos apostaticos* the rite contains a longer prayer to St. Michael followed by a series of ten conjurations, which were incorporated into the 1898 edition of the Roman Ritual:

> "Most glorious Prince of the Heavenly Army, Holy Michael the Archangel, defend us in battle against the princes and powers and rulers of darkness in this world, against the spiritual iniquities of those former angels. Come to the help of men whom God made in his own image and whom he bought from the tyranny of Satan at a great price. The Church venerates you as her custodian and patron. The Lord confided to your care all the souls of those redeemed, so that you would lead them to happiness in Heaven. Pray to the God of peace that he crush Satan under our feet; so that Satan no longer be able to hold men captive and thus injure the Church. Offer our prayers to the Most High God, so that his mercies be given us soon. Make captive that Animal, that Ancient serpent, which is enemy and Evil Spirit, and reduce it to everlasting nothingness, so that it no longer seduce the nations."

The modern Rite of Exorcism in the Catholic Church contains an express and unambiguous command addressed to the entity possessing the sick. This echoes the inherent powers granted to Christ's disciples, by which demonic spirits are said to be bound by words. Such ceremonial magic requires to be precise and exacting, and the conjurations of the exorcist are evocations of the name of the Archangel and "the Comforter" (Holy Spirit).[129] The "ancient serpent" and "profligate dragon" emanated from the Creator of the universe is summoned by reference to the pairing of the Apostles Peter and Paul amongst others, and by the adjurations and commands by the intermediary priest ("not to my own person but to the minister of Christ") and by "the might of the Holy Spirit" is cast out of the victim. The following is the command addressed to the evil spirit in the Roman Rite of Exorcism, quoted here in its entirety:

> "I adjure you, ancient serpent, by the judge of the living and the dead, by your Creator, by the Creator of the whole universe, by Him who has the power to consign you to hell, to depart forthwith in fear, along with your savage minions, from this servant of God, N., who seeks refuge in the fold of the Church. I adjure you again, + (on the brow) not by my weakness but by the might of the Holy Spirit, to depart from this servant of God, N., whom almighty God has made in His image. Yield, therefore, yield not to my own person but to the minister of Christ. For it is the power of Christ that compels you, who brought you low by His cross. Tremble before that mighty arm that broke asunder the dark prison walls and led souls forth

---

[129] John 15:26

to light. May the trembling that afflicts this human frame, + (on the breast) the fear that afflicts this image + (on the brow) of God, descend on you. Make no resistance nor delay in departing from this man, for it has pleased Christ to dwell in man. Do not think of despising my command because you know me to be a great sinner. It is God + Himself who commands you; the majestic Christ + who commands you. God the Father + commands you; God the Son + commands you; God the Holy + Spirit commands you. The mystery of the cross commands +you.

"The faith of the holy Apostles Peter and Paul and of all the saints commands + you. The blood of the martyrs commands + you. The continence of the confessors commands + you. The devout prayers of all holy men and women command + you. The saving mysteries of our Christian faith command + you. Depart, then, transgressor. Depart, seducer, full of lies and cunning, foe of virtue, persecutor of the innocent. Give place, abominable creature, give way, you monster, give way to Christ, in whom you found none of your works. For He has already stripped you of your powers and laid waste your kingdom, bound you prisoner and plundered your weapons. He has cast you forth into the outer darkness, where everlasting ruin awaits you and your abettors. To what purpose do you insolently resist? To what purpose do you brazenly refuse? For you are guilty before almighty God, whose laws you have transgressed. You are guilty before His Son, our Lord Jesus Christ, whom you presumed to tempt, whom you dared to nail to the cross. You are guilty before the whole human race, to whom you proferred by your enticements the poisoned cup of death.

"Therefore, I adjure you, profligate dragon, in the name of the spotless + Lamb, who has trodden down the asp and the basilisk, and overcome the lion and the dragon, to depart from this man (woman) + (on the brow), to depart from the Church of God + (signing the bystanders). Tremble and flee, as we call on the name of the Lord, before whom the denizens of hell cower, to whom the heavenly Virtues and Powers and Dominations are subject, whom the Cherubim and Seraphim praise with unending cries as they sing: Holy, holy, holy, Lord God of Sabaoth. The Word made flesh + commands you; the Virgin's Son + commands you; Jesus + of Nazareth commands you, who once, when you despised His disciples, forced you to flee in shameful defeat from a man; and when He had cast you out you did not even dare, except by His leave, to enter into a herd of swine. And now as I adjure you in His + name, begone from this man (woman) who is His creature. It is futile to resist His + will. It is hard for you to kick against the + goad. The longer you delay, the heavier your punishment shall be; for it is not men you are condemning, but rather Him who rules the living and the dead, who is coming to judge both the living and the dead and the world by fire." *Rite of Exorcism, Roman Ritual*

The Gospel of John alludes to these supernatural powers being wielded by the Apostles invoking Christ:

> "Very truly I tell you, whoever believes in me will do the works I have been doing, and they will do even greater things than these, because I am going to the Father. And I will do whatever you ask in my name, so that the Father may be glorified in the Son. You may ask me for anything in my name, and I will do it." John 14:12

The Roman Ritual helpfully cites indicators of spirit possession (and not merely psychological trauma) as an ability to speak in or translate tongues; the power divination; and the display of other supernatural abilities beyond the victim's age and natural condition. All these indicators are, of course, also recognised charisms of the Church, and the question must be asked as to what it is that distinguishes the two. How do we differentiate Peter invoking an angel to possess a dog and a baby from Simon's creation of a golem? How did the Seventy-Two disciples identify the evil spirits? The answer lies in intent - the exercise of virtue. The evil spirits use subterfuge, lies, and all manner of means to retain possession of their victims. For these reasons, when the Apostles failed to cast out a demon from a child, Christ told them "Howbeit this kind goeth not out but by prayer and fasting" (Matthew 17:21). This is essentially saying there is a certain type of evil spirit which cannot be driven out quickly by invocation alone, but cast out it will ultimately be. The demonic entities care nothing for the weak, the vulnerable or oppressed in society, and indeed prey on their sufferings. They do as they wilt and serve only those who offer them something in return. They operate beyond the Divine will, and therein lies the difference between the Apostles and Simon Magus:

"For thy heart is not right in the sight of God. Repent therefore of this thy wickedness, and pray God, if perhaps the thought of thine heart may be forgiven thee." (Acts 8:22)

6. Necromancy

The Resurrection of Lazarus

Necromancy is the practice of magical operations summoning the spirit of the dead or physically restoring them to life. The Jews regarded this as sinful, since God alone has power over life and death. It was also considered to be ritually taboo to come into contact with corpses, the worst form of uncleanliness. Those that did touch the dead were termed *Avi HaTum'ah* (the "fathers of uncleanliness"). Yet there is some scriptural precedent in Judaism for the practise of necromancy. Elijah raised a child from death (1 Kings 17:17-24) and Elisha resurrected the son of the woman of Shunem (2 Kings 4:32-37). The examples are few and far between, however. Jesus' raising of the dead (Jairus' daughter, the widow's son at Nain, and Lazarus) are all augurs of the Messianic Age, and demonstrations of God's power through him. They would therefore have been seen in apocalyptic terms, and far from being 'ordinary' miracles.

Necromancy is also said to be a process that allows the caster to exist in an "undead" state themselves, perhaps indefinitely, until such time as their souls incarnate into another body. In Jewish magic, the soul of the necromancer was believed to occupy an amulet contained in the small leather box containing Hebrew texts written on vellum, identical to the phylactery worn by modern Jews in prayer today. The story of Jesus' resurrection comes to mind. Is it possible that, at "the ninth hour", he entered a state of being "undead" ("It is accomplished" (John 19:30) and "Unto your hands I commend my spirit" (Luke 23:46))? Indeed, the piercing of his heart with the Lance of Longinus (the Spear of Destiny) (John 19:34) does not appear in the Synoptic Gospels. We also have the accounts of the "Harrowing of Hell"[130] which is well attested in the New Testament corpus, and the posthumous resurrection appearances themselves, hinted at in Ephesians:

> "Now that he ascended, what is it but that he also descended first into the lower parts of the earth? He that descended is the same also that ascended up far above all heavens, that he might fill all things." Ephesians 4:9-10

In contrast, there is a tradition of Simon Magus attempting to replicate this feat and failing miserably. It is recounted by Hippolytus in his *Refutation of all Heresies*, where we are told about the Magus requesting to be buried alive in the certitude of bodily resurrection:

> "When he was on the point of being shown up, he said, in order to gain time, that if he were buried alive he would rise again on the third day. So he bade that a tomb should be dug by his disciples and that he should be buried in it. Now they did what they were ordered, but he remained there until now: for he was not the Christ."[131]

Necromancy proper was the physical resurrection of a corpse. It also hints at the possibility that Simon remained in his tomb in a death-like state, since "he remained there until now." He may also, perhaps, have been weakened by his demonstrations against St. Peter, such that he made lame men walk only for a short period of time and for a little space, the blind see likewise, and raising the dead to life only briefly.[132] Simon admitted as much when he appealed to the Roman crowd for sympathy:

> "For to-morrow I shall forsake you, godless and impious that ye are, and fly up unto God whose Power I am, though I am become weak." Acts of Peter ch.32

Inasmuch that the magical operations of ancient Judaism may have survived and been incorporated into the medieval goetic texts, such as the *Grand Grimoire*, it is less likely that necromancy was among them. Commentators such as A. E. Waite identified the practice of necromancy as essentially negative and profane. Its practise in Judaism, however, is likely to have arisen out of the quest of black magicians to master Qliphothic magic as a means of mastering

---

[131] Hippolytus, *Refutation of all Heresies*, chs. 6, 15.
[132] Acts of Peter ch.32

terrestrial nature for some ultimate, higher purpose. Thus, Waite described necromancy as

> "a process ... which is possible, say some occult writers - in the geniality of a lucid interval - only to a dangerous maniac or an irreclaimable criminal" (Waite, The Book of Ceremonial Magic)

and that

> "there are even processes in Necromancy, which art is eschewed by all but the most abominable forms of Black Magic." (Waite, The Book of Ceremonial Magic, p.105).

It is the exercise of the perceived dark aspects of magic that led the Pharisees to mutter amongst themselves:

> "This fellow doth not cast out devils, but by Beelzebub the prince of the devils." Matthew 12:24

The healing in the Gospel of Matthew of a possessed, deaf and blind man was something the Pharisees regarded as within the gift of God alone. Of course, it was also a legitimate Messianic gift, but they were not going to see it that way for other reasons. However, the interesting point is that (a) they did not deny supernatural events; and (b) we learn from Jesus' response that he was also clairvoyant:

> "And Jesus knew their thoughts, and said unto them, 'Every kingdom divided against itself is brought to desolation; and every city or house divided against itself shall not stand.'" Matthew 12:25

The "amazement of the people" at the miracle demonstrates that it was being performed solely for effect. It was not necromancy, but it was certainly restorative and demonstrated Christ's complete mastery over the forces of nature. It may be said therefore that when Jesus was raising the dead proper, he was doing so in breach of the Law and a common sense of the legitimate use of magic at that time. This tells us something about the nature of his ministry, and just how radical it was. He was challenging many of the precepts of the Law, and making a statement that the Messianic Age had begun with the sign of resurrecting the dead.

Necromancy itself is a process, for want of a better word, by which life is restored to a dead body by returning the 'soul' to it. (Waite, The Book of Ceremonial Magic, p.105). Nero tells Peter that Simon Magus: "raised a dead man and presented himself on the third day after he had been beheaded." (Acts of Peter 20). There is indeed something dark and disturbing about this picture of Simon raising a man to life who has died that way, and which reflects Waite's conclusions on the practise and indeed, the colourful and diabolical descriptions found in the later grimoires. Not only does Simon's restoration of a decapitated corpse to life hark back to the murder of John the

Baptist by Herod, but it has the feel of sensationalism and blood lust about it. From what we know of Nero, the last of the Julian emperors, this should come as no surprise.

The surviving Greek magical papyri dating from around AD 400 preserve older material destroyed in the Tiberian censorship.[133] This material draws heavily from Egyptian Hermeticism. By way of example, the operations contained in the ritual of "the Headless One" (or "the Bornless" ritual)[134] which became the Stele of Jeu are interesting, because the operator invokes an entity named Akephalos, literally meaning the "Headless One". Viewed positively, this may be an invocation of the Egyptian god Ra whose head was considered to be the Sun. The text of the rite supports this hypothesis in places:

> "I summon you, Headless One, who created earth and heaven, who created night and day, you who created light and darkness; you are Osoronnophris ~ whom none has ever seen; you are Iabas; you are Iapos; you have

---

[133] See Nick Farrell https://www.nickfarrell.it: "Greek Magical papyri is a collection of different spells gathered and copied by several magicians in the late fourth century. It is a mixed bag of systems and mythologies that have been "adapted" from their original intent. They do not slot together; there is no start, middle or end. Some of the spells are based around older Ancient Egyptian religion; others are pure Greek or Hebrew. Something is a god in one area and a devil in another. The magician needs to develop a system in which the spell is incorporated to provide this consistency. Preferably this system should be one in which they have already been trained."

[134] Papyrus V.96—172

distinguished the just and the unjust; you have made female and male; you have revealed seed and fruits; you have made men love each other and hate each other.

"I am Moses your prophet to whom you have transmitted your mysteries I celebrated by Israel; you have revealed the moist and the dry and all nourishment; hear me.

"I am the messenger of Pharaoh Osoronnophris; This is your true name which has been transmitted to the prophets of Israel. Hear me, ARBATHIAO REIBET ATHELEBERSETH [AM] BMTHA ALBEU EBBNPHCHI CHITASGOB IBAOTH IAO; listen to me and turn away this daimon."[135]

However, in the Graeco-Roman world decapitation was regarded as a punishment meritorious of the worst crimes, such as murder or treason. It was also commonplace in Roman culture to bury a felon's head between his feet. It has been suggested that the "headless ones"[136] in the ancient magical rites are a genus of malevolent human spirits - hence the requirement for a rite to banish them by sympathetic magic through conjuring the headless demon. Indeed, as the ritual progresses, the mage opens himself up to possession, which is indicative of a ritual of self-exorcism. This finds support in the following text from the ritual, where the headless demon has "sight" in his feet":

---

[135] Hans Diete~Betz, *Introduction to the Greek Magical Papyri*
[136] ἀκέφαλοι, *akephaloi*

"I am the headless daemon with my sight in my feet; [I Am] the mighty one [who possesses] the immortal fire; I am the truth who hates the fact that unjust deeds are done in the world; I am the one who makes the lightning flash and the thunder roll; I am the one whose sweat is the heavy rain which falls upon the earth that it might be inseminated; I am the one whose mouth burns completely; I am the one who begets and destroys; I am the Favour of the Aeon; my name is a heart encircled by a serpent; come forth and follow."

There is therefore something diabolical in the legend of Simon Magus restoring life to a decapitated felon, albeit temporally. None of his necromancy appears to have achieved any permanence if the sources are to be believed. One has to speculate as to the identity of the deity or deities invoked by Simon for this operation, given that all goetia begins with an evocation of the spiritual genus presiding over that particular rite.[137] On another occasion, Simon manages to get the head of a dead man to move and open its eyes but fails to fully revive the entire body, causing the crowd to turn against him:

---

[137] Op.Cit Fortune p.43

Peter before Agrippa

"Then Simon went to the head of the dead man and stooped down and thrice raised himself up (or, and said thrice: Raise thyself), and showed the people that he (the dead) lifted his head and moved it and opened his eyes and bowed himself a little unto Simon ... But Agrippa the prefect had no longer patience, but thrust away Simon with his own hands, and again the dead man lay as he was before. And the people were enraged, turned away from the sorcery of Simon." Acts of Peter 28

This is not a description of mediumship, mentalism or sciomancy,[138] but the restoration of life to a dead body. Its re-ensoulment. The difference in legitimacy (that is,

---

[138] Divination through communication with the spirits of the dead.

between what we might regard as the nefarious use of magic for evil purposes, and that which is used for the force of good), is essentially what Eliphas Levy described as the discipline of virtue and right intention. I think, however, that the necromancy performed by Christ and the Apostles was essentially serving a demonstrative purpose, namely that God was present in his person, and his mission was the beginning of a new age. The Son of Man was, after all, the Second Adam and enjoyed a restoration of his dominion over the Tree of Life. This appears to be the point being made in the raising of Lazarus in the Gospel of John, because frankly the action of raising a long dead corpse was otherwise anathema to the Jews:

> "Now a certain man was sick, named Lazarus, of Bethany, the town of Mary and her sister Martha … Therefore his sisters sent unto him, saying, Lord, behold, he whom thou lovest is sick. When Jesus heard that, he said, This sickness is not unto death, but for the glory of God, that the Son of God might be glorified thereby." John 11:1-4

After tarrying two days to be absolutely sure his friend was indeed dead and beyond mortal help (noting the journey by foot was a matter of mere hours), Jesus plainly told his disciples: "Lazarus is dead." (John 11:14). When Jesus arrived, he found that Lazarus had been in the grave four days:

The Raising of Lazarus

"And Jesus lifted up his eyes, and said, 'Father, I thank thee that thou hast heard me. And I knew that thou hearest me always: but because of the people which stand by I said it, that they may believe that thou hast sent me.' And when he thus had spoken, he cried with a loud voice, Lazarus, come forth." John 11:41-43

This is necromancy proper and, without any doubt, was performed solely for effect. It also happens to be the last of Jesus' Seven Miracles in the Gospel of John. The first was when he replicated Genesis in the filling of the water jars and the transmutation into wine; and the last is the resurrection of a man who was well past surgery! Jesus lifts his eyes, gives thanks to God and Lazarus is restored. This is performed without any laying on of hands, presumably because he was too deteriorated and any confluence of spirit or vitality with the body was long gone. It was therefore a demonstration of God's supreme power over life and death through the Son of Man, the Second Adam, to whom were fully restored the three operative roots of Power, Virtue and Force. In not laying on hands, Jesus was ensuring he did not give offence to the Law.

The Secret Gospel of Mark only exists today in fragments, but we know it was being quoted as early as AD 200, around the same time as the Acts of Peter. The Secret Gospel may contain vestiges of earlier material. The resurrection of "the young man" by Jesus is so similar to the raising of Lazarus in the Gospel of John that it can only be an alternative version of the same event. In the Secret Gospel, Jesus stretches forth his arm without vocal prayer and physically touches the deceased:

> "And they came into Bethany. And a certain woman whose brother had died was there. And, coming, she prostrated herself before Jesus and says to him, 'Son of David, have mercy on me' But the disciples rebuked her. And Jesus, being angered, went off with her into the garden where the tomb was, and straightway a great cry was heard from the tomb. And going near Jesus rolled away the stone from the door of the tomb. And straightway, going in where the youth was, he stretched forth his hand and raised him, seizing his hand." The Secret Gospel of Mark

This is a demonstration of Christ's transcendental power as a sign of the coming Messianic Age. Neither should it be forgotten that Peter was present when these events occurred. Another important feature separating the raising of Lazarus from Simon Magus' activities is that of gratuity, since no money is asked for by Jesus or his Apostles, whereas Simon pointedly chooses to raise a rich Roman. As Waite points out:

> "The object of Necromantic evocations was much the same as the other operations of the Grimoires. If the sorcerer of old, like the modern magician, had ever dispossessed the shade of Apollonius of its eternal rest, it would have been upon a question of finance. The remaining process in Necromancy will be therefore an appropriate conclusion to our whole inquiry, as it is designed to raise up and expel a human spirit who is supposed to stand guard over a hidden treasure." (Waite, The Book of Ceremonial Magic, pp.325-326)

In contrast, Peter continues Christ's ministry through a utilisation of what can only be described as lawful magic applied for no personal gain. This includes reversing blindness, casting out evil demons and raising the dead (Acts of Peter 13). Esoteric medicine is effected through the application of occult forces.[139] The issue regarding Simon's magic was the source of this power. Was it being drawn from nature or from sentient, disembodied forms?

> "Here beginneth the Sanctum Regnum, called the Royalty of Spirits, or the little Keys of Solomon, a most learned Hebrew necromancer and Rabbi, containing various combinations of characters, whereby the Powers, Spirits or, more correctly, Devils are invoked, so that they are forced to appear whensoever you may determine, each one according to his faculty, and are compelled to bring whatsoever you may require of them, causing you no kind of annoyance, provided only that they are contented on their part, for these sorts of creatures give nothing for nothing."[140]

---

[139] Ibid. p.34
[140] Ibid. p.108

In Peter's case there is a direct parallel with the words and actions of Christ in his healing ministry; and we know that Peter saw his mission as part of the fulfilment of the Law – as the Apostle to the Jews. There can be little doubt that Peter's actions were legitimate Jewish magic by this benchmark. His operation is supplicatory and benevolent. The saint fully and permanently revives three people from the dead. One of these accounts is detailed:

> "And Peter lifted up his eyes unto heaven and stretched forth his hands and said: O holy Father of thy Son Jesus Christ. who hast granted us thy power, that we may through thee ask and obtain, and despise all that is in the world, and follow thee only, who art seen of few and wouldest be known of many: shine thou about us, Lord, enlighten us, appear thou, raise up the son of this aged widow, which cannot help herself without her son. And I, repeating the word of Christ my Lord, say unto thee: Young man, arise and walk with thy mother so long as thou canst do her good; and thereafter shalt thou serve me after a higher sort, ministering in the lot of a deacon of the bishop (or, and of a bishop). And immediately the dead man rose up, and the multitudes saw it and marvelled, and the people cried out: Thou art God the Saviour, thou, the God of Peter, the invisible God, the Saviour ... Go thou therefore also, O woman, and cause thy son to be brought hither and to rise again ... And she came unto the multitude, while all bewailed her; and a great crowd of senators and matrons followed after, to behold the wonderful works of God: for this Nicostratus which was dead was exceeding

noble and beloved of the senate. And they brought him and set him down before Peter. And Peter called for silence, and with a loud voice said: Ye men of Rome, let there now be a just judgement betwixt me and Simon; and judge ye whether of us two believeth in the living God, he or I. Let him raise up the body that lieth here, and believe in him as the angel of God. But if he be not able, and I call upon my God and restore the son alive unto his mother, then believe ye that this man is a sorcerer and a deceiver, which is entertained among you..."
Acts of Peter 27

If we analyse this text, we note the following apparent operations:

- Peter raises his eyes (just like Jesus);
- he stretches out his hands (just like Jesus);
- he uses words to summon God (just like Jesus);
- God grants him the power (just like Jesus);
- Peter cries the same words used by Jesus: "[Name of the deceased], come forth"; and
- the dead man is raised to life (just like… …well, you get the point).

This is neither goetia nor rule magic, and directly mirrors the raising of Lazarus. Peter's operations are purely intermediary: he is acting as a priest raising eyes, hands and prayer upwards to God, and it is this which automatically sets his work apart from Simon's. Indeed, the Magus reaches downwards in all his actions. Both miracle and magic. aver to control nature, but the former is performed *through* the operator by the power of the Holy Spirit, the Comforter. Also note the difference between Peter's raising of the dead and that of Paul in Acts 20:7-12. Paul "fell" on a dead body, embraced it, and came up again. Job done. There were no words. If we compare this with Peter's operations in the raising of Tabitha in Acts 9:36-42, we notice the same difference: Peter rose, went to the body, and prayed. He used words only once ("Tabitha, arise", mirroring Christ's simple command to Lazarus). When we consider Simon Magus' response to the crowd demanding a similar demonstration to raise the wealthy Nicostratus from the dead, he does the following:

- Simon goes to the head of the dead man (unlike Peter);
- he faces downwards (unlike Peter);
- he raises himself up three times (unlike Peter);
- he repeats "Raise thyself" three times (unlike Peter);
- Simon lifts the head and moves it (unlike Peter);
- he opens its eyes (unlike Peter); and
- Simon bows again (unlike Peter).

There is something both gruesome and ritualistic in Simon's actions, and in that it differs markedly from Peter's magic. Going to the head of the dead man is reminiscent of the Temple High Priest placing his hands on the heads of the two sacrificial goats for Azazel. This is clearly rule-based magic and a system of theurgical operation, albeit there appears to be no obvious goetic invocation preserved in the text. That said, necromancy was goetic in character, and perhaps we are simply being spared the gory details as they appear in the later medieval grimoires.

> "Then gently smiting the body nine times with the rod, he adds: I conjure thee, thou Spirit of [Name of the deceased], to answer my demands that I propound unto thee, as thou ever hopest

for the rest of the holy ones and ease of all."
(Waite, The Book of Ceremonial Magic, p.323)

This ritual is more reminiscent of Paul's raising of Eutychus in Acts, and the Old Testament resuscitations performed by Elijah (1 Kings 17:17-24) and Elisha (2 Kings 4:32-37). Elisha lay on a dead boy three times, and Elisha touched a dead boy with the staff and then lay on top of him.

The prefect Agrippa eventually tires of all this nonsense (presumably the crowd were getting bored) and shoves Simon away from the body when all signs of life in it cease, and the body is once again quite dead. The proximity of Simon in its revival is reminiscent of elemental magic, where mages typically work with just one element. Regardless, Simon is labelled a fraud, which may not be true by all accounts. We know that he complains of being drained of all energy. While there is every possibility that a successful resurrection was interrupted by Agrippa, the point of the story is that Simon does not have the same powers that Peter enjoys and is motivated by other factors.

7. Son of Perdition

The Fall of Simon the Magician
by Jacques Callot

Up to this point I have merely alluded to comparisons that may be drawn between Simon Magus and the antichrist of Christian eschatology. The modern idea of "the Antichrist" as a principle of evil or philosophical form does not fit with the beliefs of the Primitive Church. The reader will therefore appreciate with a renewed sense of insight the description regarding the "Man of Sin" or the "Lawless One":(ὁ ἄνθρωπος τῆς ἁμαρτίας (*anthrōpos tēs hamartias*).

> "Let no man deceive you by any means: for that day shall not come, except there come a falling away first, and that man of sin be revealed, the Son of Perdition." 2 Thessalonians 2:3

> "The coming of the Lawless One will be in accordance with how Satan works. He will use all sorts of displays of power through signs and wonders that serve the lie, and all the ways that wickedness deceives those who are perishing. They perish because they refused to love the truth and so be saved. For this reason God sends them a powerful delusion so that they will believe the lie and so that all will be condemned who have not believed the truth but have delighted in wickedness." 2 Thessalonians 2:9-12

2 Thessalonians is probably not an authentic Pauline epistle, but its likely composition date of around AD 80-110 places it firmly within the oral tradition of the early Church, and reflects an eschatological doctrine no doubt held by the Apostle. We read in 2 Thessalonians that the "Day of the Lord" (the Second Advent of Christ) will be preceded by the appearance of the Son of Perdition or Lawless One, who will:

- desecrate the Temple by sitting in it;
- persecute the Church[141]
- claim to be a supernatural being / show himself as a god;
- seek out worship;
- work signs and wonders "by the power of Satan";
- seduce non-believers;
- survive a fatal wound;[142] and
- be destroyed by "the spirit of Christ's mouth"

---

[141] Daniel 11:40-41
[142] Revelation 13:12

The Pauline tradition determines a dual characteristic in the unfolding of the Son of Perdition: an event or occurrence, followed by his appearance as a man impeding the second coming. Most theologians identify the event as the rise of Rome, and the Lawless One with its emperor, possibly Caligula who installed his statue on the Temple Mount. This view is reflected perhaps in the Book of Revelation, but which appears to look to a successor empire and its evil king. This may have its genesis in the depiction of the "Four Beasts" or temporal kings found in Daniel chapter 7, where one ("the little horn") shall "stand up" and who "has eyes like the eyes of a human being and a mouth that spoke boastfully." (Daniel 7:8). The elephant in the room of course is that the above attributes almost perfectly fit what we know about Simon Magus from the accounts of his career in the Acts of Peter:

- he insisted his followers remain on Mount Gerazim (the site of the Samaritan Temple);
- he persecuted the Church[143]
- he claimed to be a supernatural being and showed himself as a god (the Standing One);
- he sought out worship;
- the apocryphal accounts describe him as working signs and wonders by the power of Satan;
- he seduced non-believers;
- he initially survived a fatal fall in the Roman Forum;[144] and
- he was destroyed by "the spirit of Christ's mouth" in the supplications of Saints Peter and Paul which caused him to fall from the sky.

---

[143] Daniel 11:40-41
[144] Revelation 13:12

The critical question is not so much what constitutes miracles or magic, but whether Simon Magus can be identified with the Lawless One of 2 Thessalonians. Jesus and Simon were contemporaries. They were both from Palestine; one a Jew, the other a Samaritan. To the Jews, the Samaritans were "lawless" and which partly explains why in Matthew 10:5-10 the sending out of the Twelve excluded Samaria. They never met, but they shared a possible connection through John the Baptist. The real mystery of Simon Magus, therefore, appears to be whether the Primitive Church viewed him as part and parcel of the eschatological events building up to the Day of the Lord.

Dositheus

Perhaps the most intriguing aspect for our investigation is the existence of a man called Dositheus the Samaritan (Dositheus meaning "the Gift of God"). Dositheus was reputed to have been a follower of John the Baptist. Indeed, Clement, Epiphanius and Origen (c.AD 184-253) alike all report that Simon Magus was his pupil.

> "For after that John the Baptist was killed, as you yourself also know, when Dositheus had broached his heresy, with thirty other chief disciples, and one woman, who was called Luna — whence also these thirty appear to have been appointed with reference to the number of the days, according to the course of the moon — this Simon ambitious of evil glory, as we have said, goes to Dositheus, and pretending friendship, entreats him, that if any one of those thirty should die, he should straightway substitute him in room of the dead: for it was contrary to their rule either to exceed the fixed

number, or to admit any one who was unknown, or not yet proved." Clement of Rome[145]

Origen says that Dositheus pretended to be the Messiah:

> " ... Simon, the Magus of Samaria, and Dositheus, who was a native of the same place; since the former gave out that he was the power of God that is called great, and the latter that he was the Son of God."[146]

So, Origen tells us that Dositheus claimed to be "the Son of God". If Origen's historical sources have any credibility, then it is likely that Simon's title of "the Great One" in Acts may (perhaps) have been conferred upon him by this Dositheus, and that the root of this connection may lie within the community of John the Baptist. Given the size of the Samaritan population and the compact terrain of Samaria, the two may have been known to one another (assuming Dositheus indeed existed or lived at that time).

We need therefore to examine what the office of the Messiah meant to the esoteric community in Qumran, in order to consider how Simon may have become identified as a "false christ" by the early Christians, and if this was tantamount to being an "antichrist." If we can establish a connection, then it may be possible to argue that the "Lawless One" was Simon, to whom was falsely attributed the status of the Standing One, Son and Great Power of God. Josephus wrote that the Essenes believed in the immortality of the soul. They also rejected the Temple priesthood out of hand, and

---

[145] Clement, *Recognitions*, Book II, Chapter 8.
[146] Origen, Contra Celsum, Book VI, Chapter 11

offered their own sacrificial oblations to God instead.[147] The Essenes therefore found themselves in opposition to both the Sadducee and Pharisee factions alike. Why so? The answer lies in their rejection of the Levitical succession, and the assumption to themselves of its sacramental duties and responsibilities.

The Essenes claimed their priests enjoyed a lineage from Zadok, the High Priest during the reigns of David and Solomon. Therefore, both the Samaritans and Essenes alike refuted the Jerusalem Temple. Just like the Samaritans, the Essenes believed they were the chosen people, and not the Jews. This may explain why the Antichrist was held to seek out the desecration of the Temple. Might this also explain Christ's prophesy of its destruction, as an advent of the End Times. It was the refuters, the Essenes of Qumran, who were the sons of Zadok and moved into the wilderness to follow the true Law. Herein lies a possible connection with Simon Magus, since John the Baptist may have been booted out of the Essene community:

> "Those they have convicted of sufficiently serious errors they expel from the order. And the one who has been reckoned out often perishes by a most pitiable fate. For, constrained by the oaths and customs, he is unable to partake of food from others. Eating grass and in hunger, his body wastes away and perishes. That is why they have actually shown mercy and taken back many in their final gasps, regarding as sufficient for their errors this ordeal to the point of death." Josephus[148]

John is described in the Gospel of Mark as surviving on locusts and wild honey. He also collected about himself

---

[147] Josephus, *The Jewish War*, Book II, Chapter 8
[148] Ibid. vv.143-144

a community of followers, amongst whom may have been Dositheus and Simon Magus, in addition to Andrew, Peter's own brother. One can only speculate, but might John have been given the designation of the Great One, which in turn passed to Simon Magus?

If Simon Magus claimed to be the Messiah, what sort of messiah might that have been, and would he compare to Jesus? The War Scroll describes how the community at Qumran were preparing themselves for the eschatological conflict between God's angels and the fallen demons. Part of this expectation was the imminent coming of the prophesied Messiah. We know that Jesus' ministry and that of his first followers was focused on preparation for the imminent arrival of the Messianic Kingdom. The Essenes expected two messiahs: one a political Messiah, descended from the line of David; and the other a spiritual Messiah, descended from the line of Aaron. In Jesus we have a Davidic claimant, and in Simon of Gitta we have a possible descendant of Aaron. The latter designation may help explain his designation as the Great One or Powerful Force of God in Acts. In the apocryphal Acts of Peter, Simon is stated to have claimed: "I am the son of God come down from heaven." (Acts of Peter 15).

On the balance of probabilities it is likely that the kingdom foreseen by Jesus was supernatural. His ministry from the wilderness to the cross was in emulation of the Scapegoat of Atonement, and had a distinctly spiritual, other worldly feel to it. However, from what we know of Simon Magus, the opposite appears to be true as he was concerned with status, influence and wealth. His moral armoury was very different from that of Jesus and his followers.

The Dead Sea scroll known as *The Messianic Apocalypse* was written before AD 70. Although it predicts just the one Messiah, it nevertheless describes how the resurrection of the dead will occur at that time.

The respective powers of the Antichrist and Messiah would therefore share a focus on raising the dead. This of course is another example of the legitimate and unlawful operations of supernatural power, and it might, possibly, explain why the Essenes believed in two messiahs, the one spiritual, the other temporal and political.

The term "antichrist" only appears in the epistles of 1 and 2 John, composed around AD 85 – 100. As with 2 Thessalonians, the Johannine epistles were not written by an Apostle, but they do assume the faithful are well acquainted with the concept of the antichrist.[149] This doctrine has a closer affinity with Jesus' description of the "false messiahs" (ψευδόχριστος, *pseudokhristos*)[150] detailed in the Synoptics Gospels, the one that shall come in his name to deceive:[151]

> "I am come in my Father's name, and ye receive me not: if another shall come in his own name, him ye will receive." John 5:43

The Seven Signs

To be certain of a correlation of Simon Magus with a false messiah, we need to compare his magic with the miracles of Jesus. In Hermeticism there is always an equal and opposite balancing power. Just as the Qliphoth attaches to the Sephiroth in the Kabbalah. The raising of Lazarus was the last of the "Seven Signs" of Jesus' Messianic authority in the gospel of John. The preceding six were:

- changing water into wine at Cana

---

[149] 1 John 2:18
[150] Matthew 24:24 and Mark 13:22;
[151] Matthew 24:24; Mark 13:6, 22 and Luke 21:8,

- healing the official's son at Capernaum
- healing the paralytic at Bethesda
- feeding the five thousand (probably near Bethesda)
- walking on water in Galilee; and
- healing the man blind from birth by spitting on his eyes at the pool of Bethsaida.

Three of the Seven Signs of messiahship were acts of healing. One was feeding the hungry, and only two of the signs (changing water into wine and walking on water) were demonstrations of mastery over elemental nature. The other miracles of Jesus as recited in all four Gospels are:

- casting out an evil spirit in Capernaum (Mark and Luke)
- healing Peter's mother-in-law from fever (Matthew, Mark and Luke)
- healing the sick and exorcising the oppressed at evening (Matthew, Mark and Luke)
- the first miraculous catch of fish on the Lake of Gennesaret (Luke)
- healing a man of leprosy (Matthew, Mark and Luke)
- healing the centurion's paralyzed servant in Capernaum (Matthew and Luke)
- healing a paralytic lowered down from the roof (Matthew, Mark and Luke)
- healing a man's withered hand on the Sabbath (Matthew, Mark and Luke)
- raising a widow's son from the dead in Nain (Luke)
- calming a storm on the sea (Matthew, Mark and Luke)
- casting demons into a herd of pigs (Matthew, Mark and Luke)

- healing a woman suffering from bleeding for years as she touches his garment (Matthew, Mark and Luke)
- raising Jairus' daughter from the dead (Matthew, Mark and Luke)
- healing two blind men (Matthew)
- healing a man unable to speak (Matthew)
- healing many sick people in Gennesaret as they touch his garment (Matthew and Mark)
- healing a gentile woman's demon-possessed daughter (Matthew and Mark)
- healing a deaf and dumb man (Mark)
- feeding four thousand women and children (Matthew and Mark)
- healing a blind man at Bethsaida (Mark)
- exorcising a boy with an unclean spirit (Matthew, Mark and Luke)
- the Temple tax found in a fish (Matthew)
- healing a blind, mute demoniac (Matthew and Luke)
- healing a woman who had been crippled for years (Luke)
- healing a man with dropsy on the sabbath (Luke)
- healing ten lepers on the way to Jerusalem (Luke)
- restoring sight to Bartimaeus in Jericho (Matthew, Mark and Luke)
- withering a fig tree on the road from Bethany (Matthew and Mark)
- healing a servant's severed ear (Luke)
- the second miraculous catch of fish at the Sea of Tiberias (Luke).

Well over *half* of these miracles are acts of healing. Aside from the two which raise the dead, the remainder are evenly split between exorcisms and demonstrations of transmutative power over nature. Only a fifth of the miracles fall into this latter category. There is, of course, the resurrection and ascension. However, both were fairly common in the hagiographies of the pagan divinities at the time. Thus, there would have been no sense of incredulity at the Ascension story, nor indeed of Simon Magus' ability to fly. Let us consider in summary the signs provided to us by the heresiologists concerning Simon:

- he asserts he is a messiah;
- he later claims to be a god;[152]
- he teaches that the Demiurge created the world
- he is mortally wounded; and
- he is buried claiming he will rise again in three days.

The main difference between Jesus and Simon is the importance the former gave to the true meaning of the Law of Moses. In this he was placed firmly within the Jewish context of messianic lore. Indeed, be it the Petrine version of salvation by incorporation into Israel, or the Pauline version of justification by faith alone, there remained the belief that revelation came to humanity through Israel. Simon, a Samaritan by birth and likely influenced by the Essenes, appears to have identified messianic power as a temporal gift. We need only consider his actions and miracles to see this (as recounted in the Acts of Peter and by St. Irenaeus:

- he denied Christ: "Lo, here am I, Simon, come thou down, Peter, and I will convict thee that thou hast believed on a man which is a Jew and a carpenter's son;[153]

---

[152] Acts of Peter, ch.14
[153] Ibid. ch.14

- he performed wonderful works;[154]
- he performed "many evils with his magical charms";
- his works shall be shown to be charms and contrivances of sorcery;[155]
- he used magic and caused delusions[156]
- Satan worked in him.[157] "Thou shalt have Simon opposing thee by the works of his father";[158]
- he was described as "the angel of Satan";[159]
- he convinced a senator by his charms;[160]
- in Judaea he misleads Eubula, a woman "of honourable estate" and, "by means of a spell", took away all her gold and disappeared;
- he faked mediumship: "in dining chambers he made certain spirits enter in, which were only an appearance, and not existing in truth."[161]
- He raised the dead (temporarily);[162]
- he healed the blind and lame (temporarily)
- he made statues laugh and move; and
- he could fly[163]

For the Christian community, the risen Christ was the new Temple, and Simon's opposition to the Church was therefore a desecration of it. Simon did not "sit" in this Temple, but he rejected its validity. For the Essenes, the Antichrist was a human figure ensouled by Satan, the

---

[154] Ibid. ch.4
[155] Ibid.
[156] Ibid.ch.17
[157] Ibid. ch.5
[158] Ibid. ch.16
[159] Ibid. ch.18
[160] Ibid. ch.8
[161] Ibid.ch.31
[162] Ibid.ch.28
[163] Ibid.ch.32

"indwelling" (incarnation) scheduled to appear in conjunction with the births of the two Messiahs. Simon himself appears to have shifted from claiming to be the Great One, a messiah, to being the Standing One, a god.[164] The change occurs when he moves from Samaria to Rome. The accounts in both Acts and in the apocryphal literature are clear that he sought adulation. Like any other false messiah he demonstrated signs and wonders, seducing those outside the faith (be they Samaritan or Roman). He rejected the Law and its moral conventions, thereby raising himself beyond good and evil, since gnosis of self was both his journey and destiny.

Tellingly, Simon suffered a fatal wound long enough to be taken elsewhere by a fellow mage, and may have survived long enough for his interment while still alive (at least as described by Hippolytus). The stories seem sufficiently interwoven to at least have some plausibility. Simon's injuries and eventual death were sustained by "the spirit of Christ's mouth" i.e., the prayers of Peter and Paul causing him to fall in public. So, there is a case to be made for Simon's career as the very definition of *an* antichrist, if not *the* Antichrist.

The Antichrist

The Johannine tradition identifies plural antichrists. These are men who "went out from us, but they were not of us" (1 John 2:19). The chief characteristics of *an* antichrist in 1 and 2 John are:

- he is "a liar" who denies Jesus is the Christ;[165]

---

[164] According to the apocryphal Acts of Peter

[165] 1 John 2:22;1 John 4:3; and 2 John 7. In the Acts of Peter we read: But Simon said: Thou presumest to speak of Jesus of Nazareth, the son of a carpenter, and a

- he will appear at "the last hour";[166]
- he is "already in the world";[167] and
- he is a human being who does not seek to be worshipped or demonstrate miracles.

We can see how the second type of antichrist relates to a subversive, derogatory "false prophet" misleading the faithful by denying the mysteries of Spirit incarnate in nature.[168] These antichrists are human beings, and will appear shortly before the second coming of Christ.

Simon does share some of these characteristics. It is likely that he is a composite antichrist, or false messiah, a type of both the Pauline and Johannine perceptions. Science gives way to sorcery where there is no logical explanation of it, and in Simon's instance his actions and magic either belong to the realm of the preposterous and impossible, or else they belong to the art of real magic. In either instance, they are not within a system of ethics or an absolute principle defining the criteria of right action (be it conceived as a divine ordinance or a truth of reason, however you wish to view it). In this sense he is very much *an* antichrist, but only a false messiah to the extent that he misled others into accepting his own version of Gnosticism. It is in

---

carpenter himself, whose birth is recorded (or whose race dwelleth) in Judaea. Hear thou, Peter: the Romans have understanding: they are no fools. And he turned to the people and said: Ye men of Rome, is God born? is he crucified? he that hath a master is no God. And when he so spake, many said: Thou sayest well, Simon."

[166] 1 John 2:18
[167] 1 John 4
[168] "Who is a liar but he that denieth that Jesus is the Christ? He is antichrist, that denieth the Father and the Son." 1 John 2:22

this context that St. Peter's words as conveyed in the apocryphal Acts have resonance:

> "But in this Simon, there are two essences, of man and of devil, who through man endeavours to ensnare men."[169]

There is, finally, a third type of antichrist which does not sit comfortably with the individual known as Simon Magus. This is the version we encounter in the eschatological tradition found in the Revelation of St. John the Divine. The desecration and destruction of Jerusalem and the Temple in AD 70 by Titus, together with the depopulation of its Jewish population following the Jewish War, are examples of the quality of eschatological trauma described by John of Patmos. This Antichrist will claim to be divine and seek personal worship, but there is a clear political element that we do not see in Simon or his consort Helena. This Antichrist may relate to the "Fourth Beast" of Daniel,[170] and the "Beast of the Sea" in Revelation 13:1-2. The attributes of the Beast vary. These comprise a combination of any one or more of the following characteristics:

- "great signs and wonders" in full view of the people (Revelation 13:13);
- being a temporal leader of great worldly power (Revelation 13:5,7);
- forcing his followers to receive his mark (Revelation 13:16-17);
- violence (Revelation 19:19)
- his destruction in the "Lake of Fire".

---

[169] Ibid Acts of Peter, ch.17
[170] Daniel 7:7 and 7:23-26

The Antichrist

In the Book of Revelation, John of Patmos describes the Beast as a serpent or "dragon" with seven heads and ten horns, which he identifies with Satan (Revelation 12:9). This image of the serpent symbolizes the political dominions enslaving and repressing man's original freedoms and power. On each of the seven heads of the serpent are diadems or crowns, representing the six kingdoms (that is, Egypt, Assyria, Babylon, Persia, Greece, Rome - and an empire yet to come). Five of these kingdoms had fallen, Rome would fall, and a kingdom is yet to come. The ten horns on the dragon represent future kings of this future seventh kingdom, and who will come to power in the epoch of the Antichrist. Therefore, immanent within the Serpent was a hidden ruler of a seventh and final kingdom. Simon does not fit this apocalyptic vision, albeit his patron, the Roman Emperor Nero, might.

Concluding Remarks

I will be candid and state that, at the outset of this undertaking, my objective was to engage sympathetically with Simon Magus. I felt this approach was long overdue and that he had been dealt with roughly during the long centuries of polemic. Yet, as I progressed through the sources, I became more conscious that there was something awry with Simon, and that the Primitive Church may have had good cause to treat him with the gravest suspicion. I suspect that what lay at the heart of the matter was that distinguishing feature of Gnosticism: the rejection of sin.

The sources that resonated most were those in 1 Timothy, where the issue of wrongly passing on the charism of the Holy Spirit is juxtaposed with the twin dangers of negligent (*amelei*) and hasty (*tacheōs*) initiation through the imposition of hands:

> "Do not be negligent with the gift in you, which was given by the laying on of hands of the elderhood." 1 Timothy 4:14

> "Lay hands hastily on no one, neither be partaker of other men's sins." 1 Timothy 5:22

Peter's description of the "wickedness" of Simon hinges on the singularity of his admonition *"for thy heart is not right in the sight of God"* (Acts 8:21). This sense of anxiety over rushed initiation, and the abuse or misuse of a sacred power, amply sums up the impression that the powers of the Apostles needed to be jealously guarded. Essentially, when Simon asked for the transmission of the Holy Spirit ("Give me also this power, that on whomsoever I lay hands, he may receive the Holy

Ghost"),[171] the inference is that he intended to arbitrarily grant power (*exousian*) to whomever he wanted. There was also something that did not sit comfortably with me regarding Simon's epithets of the "Great One" and the "Great Power of God" within the context of Peter's rebuke of him. It felt almost as if Simon was already well advanced in building a following and sect of his own before Philip the Evangelist turned up, and saw the arrival of the deacon as an opportunity to consolidate his own power base by deception. Now, these passages are scriptural not apocryphal, which lends them greater credence, although what we read about Simon's antics in the non-canonical texts closely resembles the impression we receive of him in Acts.

I encountered in Simon Magus a man who appears to have lived under the doctrine "do what thou wilt." He therefore followed what occultists term "the Left Path." There is a particular problem with this choice if we, as a species, are to concern ourselves with the wellbeing and care of the weak and vulnerable. I, myself, have not been tempted to explore magic because its limits are concerned with either material gain or pleasure. A. E. Waite wrote that

> "The ambition of the Magus was to secure these advantages – firstly - by the trickery and artifice of the occult world, instead of by his proper activity, and – secondly – on a very much larger scale than was normally likely or possible."
> (Waite, The Book of Ceremonial Magic, p.319)

Simon Magus is an enigma, for sure, since we do not really know if it is the same man that is described in Josephus, let alone in the Acts of Peter and other apocryphal texts. The fragmentary accounts of him that

---

[171] Acts 8:19

are preserved in the writings of the heresiologists suggest that he might be. Simon's lofty title of "the Great One" originated from somewhere, and I doubted it was invented by Luke and gave me cause for reflection.

Whatever our view on the subject of a personal God, and whether the identity of that divinity is the God of Abraham, Isaac and Jacob, the existence of a moral Absolute guiding the path of our species and the direction of our travel is, for me at least, an important principle. It is not always a question of theism either, since the doctrine of karma or deeds in the non-theistic faiths such as Buddhism and Daoism apply similar precepts regarding the dangers of the Left Path, as there are dark magical practices and forces at play in those systems too.

When all is said and done, the influence of the Enlightenment on our present-day worldview derives from Christianity, which in turn - and in all truth - was a Jewish heresy. Ethics and morality play a central role in Judaism, whose scriptures preserve an ancient allegory of humanity's fall from perfect splendour into the encampment of a material universe. The covenant God made with a branch of our ancestors served to prepare for a moment, for a point in time when the process of healing the gulf between spirit and matter caused by man's pride and hubris could begin. In the interim, adhering to the Law was the best means of differentiating those set apart in preparation for this task. Yet in Simon Magus I found a man who was dangerous, not only in his purported abilities to manipulate nature but in his power of persuasion and charism operating without any discernible parameters. The parable of the Good Samaritan in Luke 10:25-37 is a case in mind, because as with most sacred stories, it contains an allegorical interpretation. Superficially it is about mercy, tolerance and care for the vulnerable set against a background of brutality, false piety and hypocrisy. On an allegorical level it is about right intention acting in conformity with Divine *authority*. The exoteric and esoteric versions are not so far apart, and are two sides of the same coin. As Origen wrote:

> "The man who was going down is Adam. Jerusalem is paradise, and Jericho is the world. The robbers are hostile powers. The priest is the Law, the Levite the prophets, and the Samaritan is Christ. The wounds are disobedience, the beast is the Lord's body, the inn, which accepts all who wish to enter, is the Church. ... The manager of the [inn] is the head of the Church, to whom its care has been entrusted. And the fact that the Samaritan promises he will return represents the Saviour's second coming."[172]

In the twenty-first century we do not have to accept Origen's equation of moral authority with the Church to agree that parameters are required to underpin our rules of conduct. I was recently reminded of this difference in perspectives at a recent dinner I attended, where I found myself in discussion with an acquaintance who had chosen to take up the practise of theurgy. In his own words he regarded magic as having more vitality and relevance. My own focus has always been on the mystical branch of esotericism, specifically Christian, whereas my acquaintance had embarked on a different path. The issue, as it unfolded in our conversation, was not that we differed on the ultimate goal of our endeavours, but that we disagreed on the moral parameters of that journey and what guided our actions. His newfound commitment to the art of invoking the

---

[172] Origen, Homily 34, para 3

disembodied entities of the calendar to bend to his will was troubling. Assiduously following the sigils and invocations of the kind he drew from his pocket to show me was one thing, but to reject any boundaries was quite another. "Ah, but there is a power delegated for each hour of the day, and it is the angelic entity sixty-two this evening" he said, as if that would somehow persuade me of his argument that spiritual progress depended on it. Obviously, I had to look up this particular reference later, to see exactly what it was he was invoking for his "protection" and "guidance." There are, as Aleister Crowley once said, no coincidences:

> "LXII. VALAC, a great president, comes as a little boy with the wings of an angel and riding on a two-headed dragon. He gives true answers concerning hidden treasures, tells where serpents may be seen and will deliver them helpless to the exorcist." (Waite, The Book of Ceremonial Magic, p.230)

The irony was not lost on me. A message indeed. Valac is a leader of thirty legions of demons, the invocation of which enables the mage to acquire power over them. In this I saw a direct parallel in the contrasting world views of Simon and Peter, and a direct reminder of the former's invocation of the legions of dog-like demons under Marchosias. Simon rejected the Law and its moral conventions, and raised himself beyond good and evil, since gnosis of self was both his journey and his sole destiny. His magical powers are therefore juxtaposed with St. Peter's in the New Testament, and in later writings, in order to emphasise the Apostle's authority over Simon through evocation to the Holy Spirit by following "the Right Path". Indeed, it is hubris which eventually destroys Simon, not in a Lake of Fire but from his injuries in a dark, sealed tomb. This is an ancient divergence, and one which clearly still resonates, at least for me. I dare say were the Church reduced to but one man, in all his loneliness he would still wince at Pilate's hubris when remarking "what is truth?"

I once thought the story of the three ruffians in the Hiramic legend of Freemasonry to be boring verbiage, a late eighteenth century interpolation brought in for pure drama. However, I now see the ruffians for what they are: an allegory expressing our lower selves as the true enemies of the Temple within. There is no need to practise magic or to invoke supernatural assistance to master the lower self and rebuild a functioning Temple without the use of any metallic tools. In fact, it probably delays the project. The art and purpose of Freemasonry along with most chivalric moral systems, is the development of self-awareness and improvement through repetition, practice, and living to high ideals. Invoking demons to acquire power over nature and, dare I say, to gain an upper hand over the free will of others, can never be reconciled with the Christian doctrine of grace. The God who struggled all night with Jacob across the stream of conscience will only bless those who stay the course and evolve through suffering. The legend of Simon Magus is therefore the embodiment of all the opposing vices, since there can be no greater sin than blasphemy against the Holy Spirit - which is simply to say that intentionally blocking God's grace from others is unpardonable.

It follows that Simon could no more restore the dead permanently to life any more than Solomon's men could raise Hiram Abif's dead body without a grip and embrace. Hiram's refusal to give away his secrets to those who would steal it without any reservation or care for his wellbeing is what led to his death, and it was this act of selfless chivalry which prevented his knowledge falling into the wrong hands. The Freemason is symbolically raised in the place of Hiram Abif, with the same precautionary warning as that contained in 1 Timothy: to not negligently or hastily pass on the secrets contained in the safe repository of his heart.

Now, none of this is to say that goetia and theurgy have no place at all in the spiritual evolution of humanity. There is, as I have mentioned above, a long and well-established tradition of supplicatory magic being practised within the Church. However, it is distinguished from other forms of theurgy by a reliance on moral authority. There also exists magic outside the confines of both church and synagogue which is equally legitimate, and that has been practised since humanity first descended from its tree. This is the shamanic magic practised by the hidden adepts in our communities who exorcise unclean spirits and combat the forces of evil through prayer and supplication to this very day. Their motivation is not personal gain, but reintegration with God, both for themselves and others. In this they are set apart from the New Age sentimentalism of our own time. That which they seek is a return to our original glorified state, and like the Good Samaritan they always minister to the vulnerable. One does not have to be religious to be spiritual, and neither does one have to belong to any organised faith to accept universal truths. Grace cannot be the sole charism of the Church, or of any other religious system which seeks to maintain control over Divine power. The virtues imparted by grace are those which set apart the saint from the sinner, Simon from Peter, and the false messiahs from Christ.

What is virtue in this context? It is not one thing, it is many. It is best described as positive thoughts and actions, such as those contained in the Seven Holy Virtues of Aurelius Clemens . His poem allegorises the conflict between the opposing forces of good and evil in the form of characterised "Virtues" and "Vices". It is from this tradition that we encounter Simon Magus in Dante's *Inferno*, where he resides in Hell upside down in perpetual reflection of St. Peter's crucifixion. The same St. Peter who turned around at Christ's bidding to comfort and support his beleaguered flock. This was Dante's nod to that great Hermetic truth: as above so below. At the heart of it all is the attribute of restraint. Ultimately, restraint is the foundation stone of all virtue, and that which eventually leads to true wisdom. Simon Magus appears to have had little restraint, even in the few verses concerning him in the Book of Acts.

Whether Simon existed at all, and if it is the same man we encounter in the Bible and the pseudepigraphal texts is not, ultimately, the point. The message is whether magic and miracles equate to the same thing. Clearly they do not.

Bibliography

Journal of Higher Criticism

Whiston. W., (trans.), *Flavius Josephus: The Jewish War Book III*.

Campenhausen, H. v. (1969). *Ecclesiastical Authority and Spiritual Power in the Church of the First Three Centuries*. Stanford.

Catholic Encyclopedia

Detering, H. (2003.). *The Falsified Paul: Early Christianity in the Twilight*.

Diete-Betz, H. (1997). *Introduction to the Greek Magical Papyri*. Chicago.

Edmundson, G. (1913). *The Church in Rome in the First Century*. London.

Encyclopedia Britannica. (n.d.).

F, Williams (trans.), (2009). *The Panarion of Epiphanius of Salamis*. Boston.

Fortune, D. (1930). *Psychic Self-Defence*. London.

G, W. MacRae. (2009). Thunder, Perfect Mind. *Coptic Gnostic Library, Institute for Antiquity and Christianity*.

Harari, Y. (2012). The Sword of Moses (Harba de Moshe): A New Translation and Introduction. *Magic, Ritual and Witchcraft*, University of Pennsylvania Press.

Jellinek, A. (1853). *Midrash VaVosha*. Leipzig.

Kaczynski, R. (2002). *Perdurabo: The Life of Aleister Crowley*. Berkeley.

Kohler, K. (n.d.). *Simon Magus*. The Jewish Encyclopedia.

Levy, C. (2018). *Philo of Alexandria*. The Stanford Encyclopedia of Philosophy.

MacGreggor Mathers, S. L. (1912). *The Kabblah Unveiled*. New York.

Nun, M. (1998). *Has Bethsaida Finally Been Found?*

Osborne, M. R. (2021). *The Lessons of Lyons*. London.

Osborne, M. R. (2022). *The Brazen Serpent: Order and Chaos*. New York.

Papus. (1892). *The Tarot of the Bohemians: The Most Ancient Book in the World*. Paris.

Schmidt, C. (1903). *Die Alten Petrusakten Im Zusammenhang Der Apokryphen A[pstellitteartur*. Leipzig.

Wace, P. S. (1890). *A Select Library of the Nicene and Post-Nicene Fathers of the Christian Church (2nd ed.)*. Edinburgh.

Waite, A. E. (1896). *The Ritual of Transcendental Magic by Eliphas Levi*. London.

Waite, A. E. (1898.). *The Book of Ceremonial Magic*.

Waite, A. E. (1908.). *The Holy Kabballah*.

Walsh, J. E. (1982). *The Bones of St. Peter*. London.

Index

St. Peter's Basilica, 26
A. E. Waite, 23, 34, 140, 165
Aaron, 65, 72, 139, 145, 147
Acts, 26, 36, 39, 41, 44, 45, 47, 49, 50, 52, 54, 55, 56, 57, 59, 60, 62, 65, 76, 78, 79, 80, 83, 84, 85, 86, 87, 90, 91, 92, 93, 95, 99, 100, 101, 103, 104, 105, 106, 107, 108, 116, 125, 130, 142, 144, 162, 171, 178
Acts of Peter, 144
Adam, 33, 34, 84, 111, 129, 172, 173, 200
aeons, 81
Agabus, 88, 89
Agrippa, 171, 179
Akephalos, 168
Alexandria, 33, 51, 88, 129
Alice Kyteler, 145
All Father, 120
All-Mother, 120
Almiras, 141
Andrew, 61
Angel Liturgy, 131
Angel of Death, 115, 116, 147
Appian Way, 27
Arabia Petrea, 50

Archons, 31
Ars Goetia, 134
Asaph, 146
Assiah, 129
Assyria, 196
Atzilut, 129
Avi HaTum'ah, 163
Azaezal, 66, 73
Babylon, 196
Baptism, 96
Barnabas, 91
Bartimaeus, 190
Beast of the Sea, 195
Berechiah, 146
Bethany, 172, 174, 190
Bethsaida, 9, 53, 189, 190
Black Magic, 23
Bornless, 168
Briah, 129
Caesar, 60, 89, 133, 139
Cæsarea, 42
Caesarea Philippi, 107
Capernaum, 53
Castor, 144
Celestial Hierarchy, 31, 77
Chaos, 69
charismatos, 78
church of San Sebastiano fuori le Mura, 27
Colley, 25
Confirmation, 96

Conjuration, 141
Council of Trent, 96
Crowley, 125, 201
Cyrenaica, 88
Damascus, 80, 146
Daniel, 109, 182, 183, 195
Day of Atonement. *See* Yom Kippur
Dead Sea Scrolls, 109
deceivers, 117
demiurge, 108
Demiurge, 30, 31, 32, 108, 120, 191
Demiurgos. See Demiurge
Detering, 48, 49, *See* Herman Detering
Deuteronomy, 29, 69, 74, 75, 82, 114
Dionysius the Aeropagite, 76, 77
Divine Name, 99
Divine Wisdom, 76
Dositheus, 184, 185, 187
Drusilla, 44, 118
dunamis, 35, 85, 86
Edom, 66
Egypt, 115, 116, 139, 146, 196
el-Araj, 53
Eleusinian Mysteries, 81
Eli, 39
Elijah, 92, 107, 163, 179
Eliphas Levi, 145
Eliphas Levy, 140, 172
Elisha, 92, 163, 179
Elymas, 99
emes, 75
Encausse, 127
Ennoea, 118, 119, 120, 121
Enoch, 66, 73, 109
Ephesians, 58
Ephesus, 84, 92
Epiphanius, 32, 40, 99, 124
Epiphanus, 32, 99
Essenes, 72
Eubula, 192
Eucharist, 96
Eusebius, 56, 59, 100
Eusebius of Caesarea, 100
Eutychus, 92
existato, 85, 86, 87
Exodus, 80, 114, 115, 116, 138, 139
exorcisms, 99
exousian, 83
Ezekiel, 75, 76
Father of Heresies, 47
fathers of uncleanliness, 163
Felix, 44, 118
Festus, 59
First Principle, 82
First Thought, 119
Fourth Beast, 195
Francis of Assisi, 142
Galatians, 50, 51, 56, 62, 103
Galilee, 38, 54, 70, 189
Garden of Eden, 32

Garden of Gethsemane, 60
Gardens of Nero, 26
Genesis, 34
Gennesaret, 189, 190
Gérard Encausse. *See* Papus
Gerizim Temple, 39
Gitta, 9, 37, 40, 44, 72, 145
glossolalia, 79, 84, 94, 95
Gnosticism, 116
Gnostics, 32, 105
God, 34, 75, 114, 116, 127
golem, 137, 138
Good Samaritan, 199, 203
Great One, 101, 105, 130
Great Power, 101
Great Power of God, 9, 101
Greek magical papyri, 168
grimoires, 117, 136, 137, 138
Grimorium Verum, 89
Guillaume Edelin, 145
Hades, 61
Halakhah, 29
Headless One, 168, 169
Hebrew, 61, 75, 138
Hebrews, 115
Helen. *See* Helena

Helena, 44, 99, 118, 119, 120, 121, 122, 123, 195
High Priest, 59, 66, 72, 73
Hippolytus, 81, 99, 124, 164, 165, 193
Hiram, 202
Holy of Holies, 102
Holy Spirit, 35, 63, 65, 77, 78, 79, 81, 82, 89, 90, 91, 93, 94, 95, 96, 97, 122, 129, 131, 177, 197, 201
Irenaeus, 119, 123, 125
James, 44, 58
Jannes and Jambres, 114, 115, 116
Jeremiah, 75
Jericho, 190, 200
Jerusalem, 26, 36, 39, 44, 45, 47, 50, 52, 54, 56, 58, 59, 67, 71, 72, 75, 76, 84, 89, 108, 190, 195, 200
Jewish magic, 61, 113
Jit. *See* Gitta
John, 26, 52, 53, 54, 60, 61, 62, 78, 84, 85, 91, 95, 105, 106, 107, 108, 110, 130
John E. Walsh, 26
John of Patmos, 78, 195, 196
John the Baptist, 62, 71, 84, 102, 105, 107,

108, 130, 168, 184,
    185, 186
Joseph of Cupertino,
    142
Josephus, 38, 42, 44,
    101, 109, 118, 185,
    186, 198
Jubilees, 109
Judaea, 54, 122, 192,
    194
Judah Loew ben
    Bezalel, 137
Judaism, 38, 39, 63, 73,
    74, 148
Judea, 38, 42, 44, 54, 55,
    59, 124, 145
Judges, 39
Justin Martyr, 39, 45,
    47, 49, 102, 107, 113
Justin's Martyr, 104
Kabballah, 34, 126
Kingdom of Israel, 38
Lance of Longinus, 164
Lawless One, 181, 182,
    183, 184, 185
Lazarus, 163, 172, 173,
    174, 177, 188
Lemegeton, 136
Leviticus, 65, 67, 113
Lower Regions World,
    120
Lucifer, 145
Lucifuge, 23
Lucifuge Rofocale, 23
Luke, 45, 53, 57, 60, 65,
    85, 103, 105, 142
Luna, 184

mageiais, 85
Magic, 9, 22, 23, 24,
    111, 140, 141, 145,
    147, 166, 174
magus, 39, 51, 99, 113
Malchus, 60
Man of Sin, 181
Mandaeanism, 108
Marcellus, 26, 149, 150,
    151
Marchosias, 132, 133,
    134
Marcion, 49
Marriage, 97
Maskelyne, 25
Matthew, 53, 57, 61,
    107, 130
Menander, 125
Midrash Al Yithallel,
    145
Midrash *VaYosha*, 146
Monad, 108, 119
Moses, 69, 80, 102, 114,
    115, 117, 139, 145,
    147
Mother of All, 119
Mount Ebal, 37
Mount Gerizim, 37, 39,
    46, 51
Mystery Cults, 81
necromancy, 92
Necromancy, 113, 163,
    164, 166, 167, 175
Nehushtan, 69, 145
Nero, 40, 63, 133, 134,
    139, 167, 196

Neronian Persecutions, 26
New Testament, 27, 30, 35, 39, 45, 50, 57, 60, 84, 86, 110, 115, 145, 164
Newman, 17
Nicanor, 88
Nicolas, 88
Nicostratus, 165, 176, 178
Origen, 56, 184, 185, 200
Original Sin, 143
Padre Pio, 142
Palestine, 130
Papus, 127
Pasqually, 143
Paul, 35, 40, 44, 48, 50, 56, 57, 58, 59, 62, 67, 72, 78, 80, 81, 83, 84, 88, 89, 90, 91, 92, 93, 94, 95, 99, 103, 143, 178, 193, *See* St. Paul
Pentecost, 80
Peter, 21, 26, 27, 28, 40, 41, 42, 44, 47, 51, 52, 53, 54, 55, 56, 57, 58, 59, 60, 61, 62, 63, 72, 83, 85, 91, 93, 95, 100, 106, 108, 113, 116, 131, 132, 133, 134, 139, 142, 143, 144, 148, 149, 150, 151, 152, 165, 167, 171, 174, 175, 176, 177, 179, 187, 189, 191, 193, 195, 197, 201, *See* St. Peter
phantasm, 152
Pharaoh, 139
Pharisee, 186
Philip, 34, 45, 47, 52, 54, 61, 73, 79, 84, 85, 86, 87, 88, 90, 91, 101, 104, 106, 107, 131
Philippians, 58
Philo, 109
Philosophoumena, 81
Phoenicia, 118
planōntes, 117
pleroma, 31
Primary Power, 125
Prince of Light, 132
Prochorus, 88
Pseudo-Clementine, 37, 40, 41, 103, 136, 137
Ptolemais, 88
Pulsa Denoura, 147
Pulsa Denura, 146
Qliphoth, 34, 125, 126, 129, 188
Qumran, 33, 66, 72, 106, 109, 123, 130, 132, 185, 186, 187
Rabbi Loew, 137
Rachel, 37, 41
Ramirat, 146
Revelation, 58, 78, 79, 104, 110, 133, 152, 182, 183, 195, 196
Roman Forum, 142

Rome, 26, 27, 28, 40,
    49, 54, 59, 81, 95,
    102, 103, 105, 143,
    146, 148, 149, 177,
    183, 185, 194, 196
Royalty of Spirits, 175
ruach, 71
Sabnack, 135
Sadducee, 186
sa'ir la-'Azae'zel, 66
Samaria, 38, 39, 40, 41,
    45, 52, 54, 59, 73, 84,
    85, 91, 95, 101, 104,
    109, 118
Samarians. *See* Samaria
Samaritans, 40, 72, 106,
    107
Sanctum Regnum, 175
Sanhedrin, 59
Satan, 60, 69, 129, 144,
    182, 183, 192, 196
Sea of Galilee, 53
Sea of Tiberias, 190
Second Temple, 90, 114
Secret Gospel of Mark,
    174
Sefer HaRazim, 147
sēmeia, signs, 95
serpent, 196
Serpent of Geborah,
    196
Seven Signs" of Jesus,
    188
Shekinah, 36
Shiloh, 39
Silas, 56

Simon. *See* Simon
    Magus
Simon Magus, 17, 21,
    22, 25, 26, 28, 34, 36,
    45, 53, 55, 57, 59, 61,
    63, 78, 81, 91, 92, 93,
    95, 102, 103, 112,
    116, 117, 123, 124,
    126, 129, 130, 132,
    142, 146, 149, 153,
    164, 167, 178, 181,
    184, 186, 187, 188,
    191, 195, 197, 198,
    199, 202, *See*
Simonianism. *See*
    Simonians
Simonians, 40, 82, 84,
    108, 112, 117, 119,
    121, 122, 124
Sitra Achra, 126
Solomon, 89, 99, 117,
    140, 145, 146, 175,
    186, 202
Solomon's carpet, 145
son of perdition, 181
Sons of Darkness, 132
Sons of Light, 72, 132
Sophia, 123
Soteira, 109
Soter, 34, 109, 117, 119
Spear of Destiny, 164
St. Alphonsus Liguori,
    142
St. Paul, 26
St. Peter, 21, 26, 27, 53,
    56
St. Peter's Basilica, 26

Standing One, 103, 105, 108, 109, 112, 120, 121, 185, 193
Sword of Moses, 147
Synoptic Gospels, 53
Tabitha, 178
Taheb, 46
Tau, 75, 76, 116, 145
Temple, 33, 66, 67, 71, 72, 73, 74, 95, 182, 183, 185, 190, 192, 195, 202
Tetragrammaton, 153
the Baptist, 61, 72, 85, 105, 106, 107
The Great Declaration, 81, 123, 124
The Lesser Key of Solomon, 134
The scapegoat, 67
The Thunder, Perfect Mind, 123
The Tower, 127
Thessalonians, 58, 182
three ruffians, 202
Timon, 88
Timothy, 78, 115, 116
Titus, 39
Tobit, 109
transcendental magic, 75, 142
transvection, 142
Tree of Life, 127
Universal Principle, 119, 120, 121
Vine, 135
War Scroll, 131, 132, 187
Wierus, 135
woman of Shunem, 163
Yetzirah, 129
Yom Kippur, 66, 73, 146
Zadok, 186
Zeus, 7, 120

www.ingramcontent.com/pod-product-compliance
Lightning Source LLC
Chambersburg PA
CBHW062208080426
42734CB00010B/1848